MAP 6

St. John the Baptist, a shockingly sensual painting for its time. Behind the palazzo is the aromatic Orto Botanico, a botanical garden featuring a fascinating touch exhibit for the blind. The steep walk up to the Gianicolo also rewards urban hikers with an unparalleled view of the city and its seven hills.

Across the river from Trastevere is Testaccio. This neighborhood has also preserved a tight sense of community while welcoming the bohemian movement of the moment. The least-touristed neighborhood in Rome, Testaccio boasts the greatest concentration of nightclubs and after-hours bars found within the city walls. Via Marmorata is Testaccio's main street, containing shops and restaurants like century-old Perilli trattoria and Rome's best cheese and salami shop, Volpetti. The majority of the nightlife, however, falls just south of Via Galvani in the Via di Monte Testaccio area.

Standing above the flat, more densely populated section of Testaccio, Aventino Hill is one of the lushest areas in the city. It's a perfect place for a picnic, and it also contains the Piazza dei Cavalieri di Malta with its unusual optical illusion – look through the keyhole. The houses on the hill, obviously belonging to the affluent, stand in contrast to the apartment buildings in the flats, where, until the turn of the 20th century, the tenements were connected by *ballatoi*, hanging walkways that linked cramped living quarters. Despite the neighborhood's gradual gentrification, however, much of the housing here is still inexpensive, the majority of it under rent control laws that benefit low-income families.

⭐ **SIGHTS**

BASILICA DI SAN PIETRO

The Vatican's Basilica di San Pietro (St. Peter's) stands as the symbolic and functional center of the Catholic Church. The largest church in the world, it attracts devout pilgrims, as well as secular visitors who come to admire its monumental architecture, especially the magnificent dome.

The site of the church dates back to A.D. 324, when Emperor Constantine commissioned a basilica to be built over the tomb of the first pope, St. Peter. In the mid-15th century, a new church, mandated to be the seat of Roman Catholic power, was commissioned to replace the aging original structure. Bramante, Raphael, and Michelangelo all contributed their talents to the church's design and decoration. St. Peter's was finally consecrated in 1626.

Today the basilica is Rome's most heavily trafficked tourist sight, as the long lines attest. The treasures inside include Michelangelo's bulletproof glass-encased *Pietà* and Arnolfo da Cambio's brass statue of St. Peter (pilgrims wearing the proper attire – covered midriffs and upper arms and skirts below the knees for women – may kiss its toe). The church's grand brick dome can be accessed by walking up a treacherous staircase or by taking the elevator. From the observation deck you can survey the whole of the Eternal City, while the gallery provides an aerial view of the basilica's interior.

C2 PIAZZA DI SAN PIETRO 06-69-88-47-29
HOURS: DAILY 7 A.M.-6 P.M.

SIDE WALKS

- Italian wines at Constantini
  B6 PIAZZA CAVOUR 16 •06-32-13-210
- Alfresco dinner at La Veranda del'Hotel Columbus
  C5 BORGO SANTO SPIRITO 73 •06-68-72-973
- Fonclea pub for music and conversation
  B4 VIA CRESCENZIO 82A •06-68-96-302
- Cross the Tiber via beautiful Ponte Sant'Angelo
  C5 LUNGOTEVERE CASTELLO

CAMPO DEI FIORI

At almost any hour of the day or night, this piazza is so frenetic that, approaching it from any direction, you won't even need a map to find it — just follow the noise.

The bucolic name, which means "field of flowers," gives little hint of the square's grisly history. In 1600, Renaissance thinker Giordano Bruno was burned at the stake here for heresy. (He maintained that the earth revolved around the sun and that science and philosophy should be more highly regarded than religion.) The statue of a cloaked Bruno at the center of the square stands as a solemn reminder of this grave event. In fact, his was the first of many public executions held in Campo dei Fiori until papal rule ended in 1870. Other well-known events that took place here, or near here, are no less grim. This is where the painter Caravaggio played a tennis match and, having lost, murdered his opponent on the spot. And nearby, the infamous incestuous twins Lucrezia and Cesare Borgia were born. The square's brutal history seemed to have followed the former — most of her lovers died under mysterious, and often gruesome, circumstances.

Today Campo dei Fiori is a much happier place. During the day its weekday market attracts crowds of upper-class bohemian residents who demand organic vegetables and cruelty-free household products and toiletries. At night, bars and restaurants spill out onto the piazza for a quintessentially Roman outdoor imbibing experience.

Physically, the square itself is more like a rectangle, meaning that it's long, narrow, and fairly small — not ideal for the crowds it attracts. Cars are not allowed to enter except to unload produce sold at the market.

 C3 PIAZZA CAMPO DEI FIORI
MARKET HOURS: MON.-FRI. 7 A.M.-1 P.M.

CASTEL SANT'ANGELO

Part mausoleum, part fortress, and part prison, Castel Sant'Angelo is Rome's most imposing intact architectural structure. Gripping the northern edge of the Tiber's elbow, this enormous circular slab of rock once protected popes during times of war and invasion; today it guards a rich history that dates back to the 2nd century.

In A.D. 135 Emperor Hadrian commissioned this building to be his mausoleum, and it was completed five grueling years later, under the watch of his successor, Antonius Pius. Between A.D. 500 and 1500, it served as a fortress for the city's papal leaders — it even had a corridor built in the 13th century that connected the castle to the Vatican. The building received its current name in A.D. 590, when Pope Gregory the Great reported seeing an angel on the roof of the castle. In the vision, the angel was sheathing his sword, an act that Gregory interpreted as a divine sign that the plague raging in Rome was over. (The bronze statue standing at the castle's summit materializes the substance of Gregory's vision; its metallic surface often catches the sunlight at various times of the day, making the building all the more formidable as a city landmark.)

Periodically during its history, the castle was also used as a prison and, no doubt, a torture chamber. Giordano Bruno, the "heretic" burned at the stake in 1600, was incarcerated here, as was Beatrice Cenci, who became the protagonist of Percy Bysshe Shelley's verse drama *The Cenci,* which is still performed every year in Roman theaters.

After crossing the former moat to the building, visitors to Castel Sant'Angelo will first encounter the original door to Hadrian's tomb. Once inside, a ramp leads to the cell where the 2nd-century emperor's ashes were kept. The papal apartment in the tower is also open to the public. Much more elegant than one might imagine, the residence is decorated with 16th-century frescoes that hint at the luxury the popes of the day demanded. Finish with a visit to the upper terraces, which afford sweeping views of the city below.

 C5 LUNGOTEVERE CASTELLO 50 · 06-39-96-76-00
HOURS: TUES.-SUN. 9 A.M.-8 P.M.

CATACOMBS

In the 5th century B.C., a religious mandate prohibited burials inside the city walls; as a result Romans interred the dead in underground cemeteries, or catacombs. In fact, more than 200 miles of tombs lie beneath Via Appia Antica in southwest Rome. Over the years, some of the excavated bones have been moved to other locations, but the majority has remained in place for centuries. Dim and macabre, the catacombs provide a unique glimpse into the rituals associated with the end of life in ancient Rome.

Although there are also Jewish and pagan catacombs under suburban Rome, the Christian burial sites draw the most visitors, and of these the Catacombs of San Callisto and San Sebastiano are the most popular. In these tombs, bodies were typically embalmed, wrapped in linen, and placed in a custom carved shelf built into the soft volcanic rock under the city. These shelves were then sealed with marble. Wealthy families were buried together, and their tombs often include religion-themed frescoes.

The Catacombs of San Callisto are the oldest and best-preserved in the city. Many popes are buried here, and the inscribed Crypta dei Papi is part of the tourable area. Farther down the Appian Way are the San Sebastiano Catacombs, which played an important role in expanding the popularity of these underground cemeteries. In the 4th century, St. Sebastian became a heroic martyr for the persecuted Christians, and his burial site became an object of pilgrimage, even into the Middle Ages. (The term "catacomb" actually comes from references to his tomb's address as "near the hollow," or *catacumbas* in ancient Greek.) Today casual visitors and pilgrims alike can see the crypt around his tomb, as well as the *triclia,* which may have briefly housed relics of Sts. Peter and Paul.

OFF MAP SAN CALLISTO: VIA APPIA ANTICA 110 • 06-51-30-15-80
HOURS: DAILY 8:30 A.M.-12:30 P.M., 2:30-5 P.M.

OFF MAP SAN SEBASTIANO: VIA APPIA ANTICA 136 • 06-78-87-035
HOURS: FRI.-WED. 8:30 A.M.-12:30 P.M., 2:30-5 P.M.

COLOSSEO

As iconic to the Eternal City as the Empire State Building and the Eiffel Tower are to New York City and Paris, the Colosseo embodies ancient Rome, standing as a reminder of its glory and ingenuity, as well as its excesses and cruelty.

Built by Emperor Vespasian in A.D. 72, the Colosseum could hold more than 50,000 spectators for its "sporting events." The design made use of engineering advances of the time, such as the familiar Roman arch, and even included a cover to shield the audience from rain and sun. Sails from the imperial fleet were elaborately rigged over the whole structure and controlled by sailors themselves. (In fact, the whole operation was so successful that it is the basic model used for entertainment and sports arenas today.)

However, far more than its architectural accomplishments, the Colosseum is known for the spectacles that were held within its arena. Gladiators fought wild animals and each other for the entertainment of powerful politicos, mostly emperors and senators. During combat exhibitions, a winner was declared only after his opponent had been slaughtered. The injured who could no longer fight were often put to death; the bodies were then prodded with hot irons to make sure that no one was feigning lifelessness.

Human gladiator fights ended in A.D. 404, and Romans tired of all their grisly games around the 6th century. They subsequently began looting the massive edifice for stone and marble to use in other grand construction projects. This went on until 1749, when Pope Benedict XIV consecrated the remains of the Colosseo as a church.

Today this famous collapsed cake-like structure functions primarily as an attraction, drawing long lines of visitors. The city may also start using parts of the Colosseum once again for entertainment purposes, although anything will surely be tame by ancient standards.

 D3 PIAZZA DEL COLOSSEO 06-39-96-77-00 OR 06-70-05-469
HOURS: DAILY 9 A.M.-6 P.M.; DAILY 9 A.M.-3:30 P.M. (WINTER)

FONTANA DI TREVI

Completed in 1762, Fontana di Trevi is the most famous fountain in a city known for its fountains. Anita Ekberg immortalized it in Fellini's *La Dolce Vita,* and wishful visitors deposit hundreds of dollars a day into its pool.

The excitement is understandable, as Nicola Salvi's roiling rococo images of Neptune, gargantuan winged horses, and conch-blowing tritons are extravagantly designed. Reliefs surround the central sculpture; one depicts a young virgin who had led thirsty soldiers to the fountain's source. (This spring was thereafter called Acqua Vergine.) Urban legend has it that the girl's name, Trivia, gave rise to the fountain's moniker. Historians, however, believe that the name more likely comes from the fountain's location at the junction of three roads, or *tre vie.*

Another of the Trevi's legends states that if you throw a coin into the fountain, you are guaranteed a return to Rome. The money left behind by visitors is collected every Monday and donated to a local AIDS hospice. Roberto Cercelletta, a local jobless man, also appears to have shared in the fountain's bounty — he boasted publicly of having removed $300 a day from the pool for 34 years until his arrest in 2002.

To get to the fountain, follow the signs from Via del Corso. Narrow streets will lead you to this small piazza that is always filled with camera-toting tourists. Sometimes during the lunch and dinner hours, you can get close enough to stick your foot in, but don't try to go any deeper. Would-be Anita Ekbergs are fined on the spot.

3 **F4** PIAZZA DI TREVI

SIDE WALKS

- Coffee at historic Antico Caffè Greco
  D4 VIA CONDOTTI 86 • 06-67-91-700
- Get coiffed at Femme Sistina
  D4 VIA SISTINA 75A • 06-67-80-260
  - La Terrazza dell'Eden for a romantic dinner
    D5 VIA LUDOVISI 49 • 06-47-81-21
- Cocktails at Gilda
  E4 VIA MARIO DEI FIORI 97 • 06-67-84-838

FORO DI TRAIANO

In its day, Trajan's Forum was the grandest of all Roman forums. Standing next to Trajan's Markets and containing a basilica, libraries, and other civic buildings, this center represented a hub of daily life in ancient Rome.

Apollodorus of Damascus designed Emperor Trajan's grandiose forum, and the slaves at his command constructed it in A.D. 112. Built and decorated with the finest marble, the complex boasted beautiful buildings that were still impressive 200 years later when Emperor Constantine was reportedly awestruck upon seeing them. The adjacent markets, a multilevel shopping center, also flourished with vendors occupying its more than 150 stalls and residents gathering at Rome's first wine bars. Archaeologists have discovered evidence of saltwater tanks in the markets, leading them to believe that fishmongers sold their catch alive.

When touring these ruins, don't miss the exedra, a gigantic curved wall with seating underneath that accommodated both private and public meetings. The markets remain a wonder of ancient architecture as well, and within you can see the sheer number of vending stalls. Also on the site is a defensive tower that was built much later, in the 13th century, for Pope Gregory IX. After many years of restoration work, this structure is now open to the public.

5 **B2** VIA IV NOVEMBRE 94 • 06-67-90-048
HOURS: TUES.-SUN. 9 A.M.-6 P.M.

 SIDE WALKS

• Imagine Nero's Golden House that used to stand at Domus Aurea
C4 VIA DELLA DOMUS AUREA • 06-36-96-77-00

• Galleria Doria Pamphilj's Caravaggio paintings
B1 PIAZZA DEL COLLEGIO ROMANO 2 • 06-67-97-323

• Check out the smoked fish selection at La Corte
B1 VIA DELLA GATTA 1 • 06-67-83-842

• Catch a local music act at I Vitelloni
D4 VIA SAN GIOVANNI IN LATERANO 142 • 34-74-47-81-67

FORO ROMANO / MONTE PALATINO

The symbolic heart of the Roman Empire, the Forum held all that enabled the conquests of Greece, Sicily, and Carthage. Complete with shopping areas, gathering places, courts of law, and government offices, it was the center of social life in republican Rome.

Unlike many other Roman monuments, the Forum was not built from one imperial vision or decree, but rather, it evolved. The physical geography – a valley enclosed by Rome's famous seven hills – made it a natural meeting spot. Successive reigning powers – the Etruscans, the Republic, the emperors – each elaborated on the site until the decline of the Roman Empire.

Today, what remains of the original Roman Forum leaves much to the imagination, in part because Romans themselves pillaged the structures for construction materials. The chief sights include the arches of Septimius Severus and Titus, both erected to celebrate war victories. Also, the Comitium is the large open space where political orations were delivered and Romulus's burial site of legend.

South of the Temple of Antonius and Faustina, the best-preserved ruin in the Forum is the small but impressive Temple of Vesta, where vestal virgins (the government's kept women, so to speak) once guarded the sacred flame. The Via Sacra, the dirt path that winds through the site, is itself of interest; wagon tracks and stones from the original roads are still visible in patches along the way.

An average visit to the Forum takes at least an hour. You can buy an audio guide and a site map at the ticket office to help flesh out the details of life during the heyday of the empire. To get a view of the Forum that once only emperors and papal families enjoyed, walk up to nearby Monte Palatino, accessed via the Arch of Titus. This hill is also believed to be the site where Romulus founded Rome in 753 B.C.

 C2 FORO ROMANO: VIA DEI FORI IMPERIALI 06-69-90-110
HOURS: DAILY 9 A.M.- 4:30 P.M.; DAILY 9 A.M.- 6 P.M. (SUMMER)

 D2 MONTE PALATINO: VIA DI SAN GREGORIO 20 • 06-69-90-110
HOURS: DAILY 9 A.M.- 4:30 P.M.; DAILY 9 A.M.- 6 P.M. (SUMMER)

MUSEI VATICANI/CAPPELLA SISTINA

Surpassing the pasta, la dolce vita, and perhaps even the ruins, the world's most famous ceiling is the crowning highlight of a visit to Italy for thousands of people every year. And with good reason: the Sistine Chapel's 10,000 square feet of frescoes by Michelangelo are among the Western world's most impressive art.

Michelangelo began work in 1508, painting the scenes in reverse order, and the entire project took him four years to complete. Because he had to work alone upon scaffolding while lying on his back, he remarked that for many years after the chapel was completed, he couldn't read anything without holding it up over his head. Nevertheless, he returned 24 years later to paint the altar wall with the final scene, The Last Judgment. During the early 1990s, expert restorationists cleaned and restored the chapel's frescoes. Their work remains controversial because the color of the images is much more vibrant than it had been for hundreds of years.

In order to gain admittance to the chapel, visitors must enter and walk through the Vatican Museums, the equivalent of 4.5 miles of exhibits. It takes a minimum of one hour, and up to four, to arrive at the chapel after purchasing tickets at the Vatican Museum entrance. This long prelude is hardly an endurance test of the faithful, however; the museums are themselves important and fascinating. The collections in this vast compound range from Egyptian art to 16th-century maps to pagan antiquities, with countless sculptures in between – including the world's largest accumulation of classic statues.

The mandatory trip through the Vatican Museums makes entering the Sistine Chapel even more dramatic. Images cover the entire ceiling of the chapel and one wall, and they tell the story of humankind before the birth of Christ through nine primary panels. The ceiling frescoes portray, in order from the altar, the Separation of Light from Darkness, the Creation of the Heavenly Bodies, the Separation of Land and Sea, the Creation of Adam, the Creation of Eve, the Fall of Man and the Expulsion from Paradise, the Flood, the Sacrifice of Noah, and the Drunkenness of Noah.

 B2 VIALE VATICANO 06-69-88-38-60 OR 06-69-88-43-41; 06-69-88-45-87 (TOURS)
HOURS: MON.-FRI. 8:45 A.M.-4:45 P.M.; LAST SAT. AND SUN. OF THE MONTH 8:45 A.M.-1:45 P.M. (NOV.-FEB.)

PANTHEON

From the outside, the Pantheon appears majestic, but in a quieter way than other buildings in the ancient city of Rome. It is the interior that reveals the Pantheon's importance as a feat of architectural genius. There is a precise harmony in the structure's dimensions: The radius of the dome is exactly equal to its height, which means that it could accommodate a perfect sphere.

Once a pagan temple by Agrippa, the Pantheon took its current form around A.D. 120, when Hadrian completely rebuilt it on the site of the original structure that had been completed only a hundred years earlier. Because Hadrian left the inscription over the entrance that attributes the structure to Agrippa, historians were confounded for many years as to the building's origins. Then, in 1892, archaeologists discovered that each brick used in the construction of the Pantheon is stamped with the date A.D. 120.

Over the years, the site has become an important burial place. The Renaissance painter Raphael is entombed here, as are King Vittorio Emanuele II, unified Italy's first king, and King Umberto I. Also it is the best-preserved architectural structure of Imperial Rome, largely due to its acquisition by the church in 608. (Despite this, various popes had allowed it to be pillaged for other building projects. The most famous instance occurred in the 1620s, when Pope Urban VIII instructed Bernini to take all the bronze covering the wooden beams of the portico for use at St. Peter's.)

It is easy to forget that the Pantheon is actually a church, unless you happen upon a service. But standing in the center of the dome can be a religious experience, especially upon noticing the hole in the top. This orifice is meant to be a symbolic connection between heaven and earth, but it is also a literal source of light as the Pantheon's sole illumination.

 C10 PIAZZA DELLA ROTONDA 06-68-30-02-30
HOURS: MON.-SAT. 8:30 A.M.-6:30 P.M., SUN. 9 A.M.-6:30 P.M.

PIAZZA DEL CAMPIDOGLIO/ MUSEI CAPITOLINI

 Capitoline Hill – known as the Campidoglio in Italian – was the most important of Rome's seven hills and has been the headquarters of civic government since the city was founded. Today, the elaborate Michelangelo-designed Piazza del Campidoglio lies at the center of a horseshoe of buildings that house both art and politics.

As early as the 6th century B.C., the Etruscans had established the hill's importance by building upon it temples to Jupiter (the symbolic father of the city), Minerva (the goddess of wisdom), and Juno (the city's guardian goddess). Two millennia later, in 1537, Pope Paul III commissioned Michelangelo to design the Piazza del Campidoglio as a matter of civic pride – the area had become a mess of goats and mud – occasioned by the visit of Charles V.

The most dramatic approach to the piazza is via the grand ramp, or *cordonata,* that sweeps up the hillside. At the top of the steps is Palazzo Senatorio, City Hall, built by Giacomo della Porta and Girolamo Rainaldi after a Michelangelo design. The buildings that flank either side of the Senate, Palazzo Nuovo and Palazzo dei Conservatori, together form the Capitoline Museums. A donation from Pope Sixtus, one of the papacy's greatest art patrons, started these vast collections of classical sculpture. Highlights from both buildings include *Dying Gaul, Capitoline Venus* (Cleopatra), and *Marble Faun* (which inspired Nathaniel Hawthorne's novel of the same name). In addition, the famous pieces from the statue of Constantine – an enormous head and pointing hand, among others – stand in the courtyard of Palazzo dei Conservatori. Among the museum's painted treasures are Caravaggio's *La Buona Ventura* and *San Giovanni Battista* and Rubens' *Romulus and Remus.*

 C1 INTERSECTION OF VIA DEL TEATRO DI MARCELLO, VIA DELLE TRE PILE, VIA DEL CAMPIDOGLIO, AND VIA SAN PIETRO IN CARLERE 06-67-10-20-71 MUSEUM HOURS: TUES.-SUN. 9 A.M.-7 P.M.

PIAZZA DI SPAGNA

The hub of Rome's most famous shopping district, Piazza di Spagna sits at the convergence of Via Condotti and Via del Babuino, streets crowded with designer boutiques, outdoor cafés, and well-heeled tourists of all ages and nationalities. The tourist-weary may quickly point out this sight's shortcomings — the throng of shoppers, shutterbugs, and young backpackers that clog the area day and night and the conspicuous absence of locals — but the history and sheer aesthetic beauty of the plaza and its famous steps are undeniable.

Built in 1723, the Spanish Steps connect the piazza with the French church Trinità dei Monti at the top. However, they were named after the Spanish Embassy to the Vatican, which also occupies the summit. In the early 1800s, the steps became the stomping grounds of the romantics when Keats and Shelley moved into the neighborhood.

With their cascade of stone staircases and the twin church towers rising above, the steps are striking at any time of year, but they are most glorious around Easter. This is when huge pots of blooming azaleas adorn the flights and terraces, and wisteria purple the side streets that lead to the steps from the top. (Unfortunately, this is also among the most popular times to visit the steps — they will never be empty for that perfect photograph unless the square is blocked off for some official function.)

A visit here will naturally include an amble up or down the stairs and perhaps some time perched on a step for international people watching. You can also see the apartment where Keats died of tuberculosis in 1821, now a museum on the plaza (Piazza di Spagna 26). For an extension of the literary theme, stop in at the nearby Caffè Greco, which has hosted the likes of Goethe, Wagner, Stendhal, and Baudelaire.

 D4 INTERSECTION OF VIA DEL BABUINO, VIA CONDOTTI, AND PIAZZA TRINITÀ DEI MONTI

PIAZZA NAVONA

 Surrounded by countless retail shops, wine bars, and restaurants and filled with tourists and locals alike, Piazza Navona is a centerpiece of life in Rome. Abuzz with energy, this place is about beauty and conversation, as well as history.

The large, rectangular square is often thought to be the most beautiful in Rome, in no small part because of Bernini's magnificent baroque fountains. In the middle, with a dramatic obelisk, is the Fontana dei Fiumi; its stone figures represent the four main rivers of the world that were known at the time. Facing out toward these masterpieces, cafés filled with lingerers line the square and earn the piazza its reputation for being the most laid-back in Rome. Nearby, shops cater to a variety of consumers who can get clothing and household goods for a fortune or a song.

The spirit of the piazza is perhaps best embodied by a truncated statue of Pasquino, a neighborhood cobbler for the Vatican who was known for his predilection for gossip. He is memorialized in the southwest corner of the main square with a little piazza of his own, Piazza Pasquino, and seems an appropriate guardian of a place that's all about socializing.

Despite its conspicuous display of all the trappings of modern life, Piazza Navona manifests its historic layer in the narrow cobblestone streets that now form the pedestrian arteries leading to the square. Most of the city's antique stores are here, and the general solemnity along the way hearkens back to the times when the area was used as a training ground for future warriors. On the southwest side of the piazza, Borromini's Church of Sant'Agnese in Agone also bears a bit of the ancient — it sits on the site where, according to legend, St. Agnese was burned at the stake A.D. 304 for refusing to abjure Christ.

 C7 INTERSECTION OF VIA AGONALE, CORSIA AGONALE, VIA DELLA CUCCAGNA, AND VIA DI SANT'AGNESE

SAN CLEMENTE

Boasting a complete medieval interior, dramatic frescoes, and structures that date back to the 2nd century, the church of San Clemente is a fascinating architectural, artistic, and archaeological sight.

The third church to be built on this site, the current San Clemente was built in 1108 and incorporates features of the 4th-century and 2nd-century structures that came before it. The marble panels near the altar came from the second incarnation of the church and are painted with doves, fish, and vines – symbols of the early Christian church. St. Clement, for whom the church is named, is also buried here, in a sunken tomb at the front of the altar. Also on this first level are the 15th-century frescoes on the left wall, which tells the story of St. Catherine of Alexandria, and a colorful 12th-century mosaic depicting biblical scenes.

Below the current church lies the second of the three buildings. The Irish Dominicans (the order that is charged with the care of San Clemente) began excavations of the previous structures in 1857. The 4th-century church is fairly well preserved, perhaps because its discovery was relatively recent. On this level dim frescoes recount the legend of St. Clement, Italy's fourth pope, who was exiled to Crimea by Emperor Trajan.

Underneath the 4th-century ruins is yet another layer of history, a 2nd-century structure thought to be a shrine to the cult of Mithras. This was the only pagan religion that seriously rivaled Christianity and also the only one that had not been disbanded after Rome officially chose to follow Christianity in A.D. 382. These ruins are not as well preserved as the ones above, but you can still get a clear sense of the layout of the space in which secret rituals and celebratory banquets were held.

 D4 VIA SAN GIOVANNI IN LATERANO 06-70-45-10-18
HOURS: MON.-SAT. 9 A.M.-12:30 P.M., 3-6 P.M.; SUN. 10 A.M.-12:30 P.M., 3-6 P.M.

SANTA MARIA IN TRASTEVERE

Among the innumerable similarly named churches in Rome, Santa Maria in Trastevere holds the distinction of being the first church in Rome ever to have been dedicated to the Virgin Mary. Built before the 4th century A.D., it is also one of the city's oldest places of worship.

The church you see today is the result of major renovations in the 12th century. On the exterior, the mosaics on the façade are of particular interest. These include depictions of Mary breastfeeding the baby Jesus, along with 10 crowned women holding lanterns against a gold backdrop – particularly stunning at night when the church is lit up.

Inside the church, Pietro Cavallini's *Madonna and Child*, and fragments of rare 1st-century mosaics from Palestrina are on display, along with an equally rare wooden painting of the Madonna from the 6th century. Between the church's windows, Cavallini also depicted the life of the virgin in mosaic. Look under the figure of the Virgin Mary in the nativity scene to see a little box with a stream of oil running from it. This installation memorializes the legend that oil flowed from the piazza on the day of Christ's birth.

As the center of the main piazza in Trastevere, the church also hosts vibrant celebrations, outdoor concerts, and other cultural events, drawing as many locals as tourists.

6 **B3** PIAZZA SANTA MARIA IN TRASTEVERE 06-58-14-802
HOURS: DAILY 8 A.M.-1 P.M., 4-7 P.M.

SIDE WALKS

• Lush gardens of Orto Botanico
A2 LARGO CRISTINA DI SVEZIA 24 • 06-68-64-193
• Light reading at The Corner Book Shop
A3 VIA DEL MORO 45 • 06-58-36-942
• Sweet treats from Valzani
A4 VIA DEL MORO 37B • 06-58-03-792
• Enoteca Ferrara for a casual dinner
A3 VIA DEL MORO 1A • 06-58-03-769

TERME DI CARACALLA

The ritual of bathing in ancient Rome was not unlike the spa culture in the U.S. today — both involve relaxation through cleansing. However, in ancient times, fees for access to the baths were nominal (everyone but slaves could afford them), and soap had not yet been invented. Upon their completion, the Baths (Terme) of Caracalla were the largest ever built in Rome, and they remained open until the 6th century.

In A.D. 206, Emperor Septimius Severus began building the baths and his son, Caracalla, completed them. The facilities could accommodate 1,600 bathers simultaneously, as the Romans were not as concerned with privacy as 21st-century spa-goers. In fact, bathing was a social activity. The process started by working up a sweat in the *sudatoria,* something like a sauna. Next came the *calidarium,* a communal sweat lodge of sorts that was both hot and humid. Since there was no soap, scrapers were used for the job of removing dirt — the wealthy usually paid someone to do this for them. The *tepidarium* was, as the name suggests, a room for cooling down slowly, whereas the *frigidarium* was more like a cold plunge-pool.

Typically the baths were open from midday until sunset. The complex included two large gyms where visitors could exercise before their baths. There were common areas and gardens for strolling, as well as art galleries, concert halls, and libraries.

The current site only hints at what was here before. Still standing are parts of stone walls that once designated the *frigidarium, tepidarium,* and other exercise and meeting spaces. Mosaics can also be seen in the gymnasiums. The informative audio-guides help fill in the gaps, while an active imagination will do the rest.

OVERVIEW MAP E4 VIA DELLE TERME DI CARACALLA 52 • 06-57-58-626
HOURS: DAILY 9 A.M.-6 P.M. (APR.-SEP.); MON. 9 A.M.-1 P.M.;
TUES.-SUN. 9 A.M.-3:30 P.M. (SEP.-MAR)

VILLA BORGHESE/GALLERIA BORGHESE

The most beautiful park in all of Rome, the Villa Borghese is akin to Hyde Park in London and Central Park in New York City for its inextricable place in the hearts of city-dwellers. In addition to its recreational open space and landscaped gardens, the park is home to Galleria Borghese, one of Rome's finest collections of art.

The brainchild of Cardinal Scipione Borghese, a 17th-century hedonist and the beloved nephew of Pope Paul V, the Villa Borghese began as a garden that included vineyards, exotic plants, and Mediterranean fruit trees. The appearance of the current park is mostly the work of Jacob More, an 18th-century painter hired to transform the gardens from their formal but asymmetrical style to a more natural style favored by the British at the time. When Rome became the capital of unified Italy in 1870, Scipione's descendants tried to sell the property to developers, but the city stepped in and, after a long and bilious legal battle, secured the park for public use.

Modern-day Romans use the expansive grounds for jogging, biking, and picnicking. In-line skates, bikes, electric scooters, and leg-powered carts can be rented within the park. Public events are held at an amphitheater in Piazza di Siena, and there's also a horseback-riding ring, a movie theater, and even a lake complete with quacking waterfowl.

Standing on the eastern side of the park is the Borghese family's former summer party mansion. Built in 1613, this structure now houses their private art collection. This sumptuous selection of sculptures and paintings includes works from many of Italy's masters: Bernini, Caravaggio, Raphael, Rubens, and the like. There's also a café inside, a good place to stop for an espresso to help digest this feast for the eyes.

 C6 VILLA BORGHESE: MAIN ENTRANCE AT PIAZZALE BRASILE

 A1 GALLERIA BORGHESE: PIAZZALE SCIPIONE BORGHESE 5 · 06-32-810
HOURS: TUES.-SUN. 9 A.M.-7:30 P.M.

® RESTAURANTS

DIRECTORY OF RESTAURANTS

AFTER HOURS

BREAKFAST AND BRUNCH

BUSINESS

CAFÉS

DÉCOR

AFRICA

This unassuming restaurant attracts pasta-weary Romans. Specialties include *zighini* (spicy beef) and *sambussa* (minced meat logs), which are eaten, as are all dishes here, with *injera*, a spongy, absorbent, sour bread. It's also open for traditional yogurt-based breakfasts, a welcome change from the usual sweet pastries. $

 D3 VIA GAETA 26
06-49-41-077

AGATA & ROMEO

In an inauspicious neighborhood near Termini Station, Agata and Romeo Parisella quietly serve some of Rome's best *cucina nuova*, which never loses sight of its local roots. The menu changes monthly and reflects the market offerings, which might include organic string beans or locally caught fish. Two tasting menus offer great value. $$$

 F3 VIA CARLO ALBERTO 45
06-44-66-115

ALBERTO CIARLA

Perpetually vying for the crown of top fish restaurant in the city, Alberto Ciarla is from a bygone era. Servers are formal and eminently versed in the day's catch and its subtle preparation, often as simple as sea bass with fresh herbs. $$$

 C3 PIAZZA SAN COSIMATO 40
06-58-18-668

AL BRIC

On the whimsical menu at this intimate restaurant, you might find hot-and-sour Thai soup next to home-made tagliatelle with *fior di zucca* (zucchini blossoms). Owner Roberto Marchetti promises that the often organic ingredients are the freshest available, and his extensive wine list is a bargain. $$

 B2 VIA DEL PELLEGRINO 51
06-68-79-533

AL POMPIERE

A sleeper in a neighborhood full of trendy dining spots, Al Pompiere hasn't changed in decades. Roman and Jewish traditions rule here: fried *baccalà* (salt cod) and *strachetti* (a sort of jerked beef) with arugula are among the menu's staples, which are served with informality and cheer. $$

 E5 VIA SANTA MARIA DEI CALDERARI 38 •06-68-68-377

L'ANTICA BIRRERIA PERONI

At this *birreria* of Italy's most exported beer, you can try all the brews not available worldwide, like the Gran Riserva, a voluptuous beer that goes perfectly with the hearty Tirolean food served here. The space is a true beer hall, with communal seating. $

 A1 VIA DI SAN MARCELLO 19
06-67-95-310

ANTICO ARCO

This hideaway near Gianicolo hill draws locals interested in exploring international wines (at fair prices) paired with inventive food such as onion soup made with parmigiano-reggiano cheese. Servers are among the friendliest in town. $$$

 B1 PIAZZALE AURELIO 7
06-58-15-274

▲

ANTICO CAFFÈ GRECO

Once a favorite of Romantics Byron, Shelley, and Keats (who lived around the corner in Piazza di Spagna), this café is now filled with shoppers from the Via Condotti. A cappuccino here, at $8, is perhaps the most expensive in town. Elegantly displayed *tramezzini* (the Italian equivalent of finger sandwiches) tempt the hungry. $$

 D4 VIA CONDOTTI 86
06-67-91-700

ASINOCOTTO

The only openly gay-owned restaurant in Rome welcomes gourmets of all persuasions with cutting-edge dishes like zucchini blossoms stuffed with green ricotta and homemade chocolate gelato with celery syrup. Wines by the glass are especially well chosen to reflect

Italy's regions and accompany the light menu. **$$**

 B5 VIA DEI VASCELLARI 48
06-58-98-985

ATM SUSHI BAR

More Japanese than Italian, this sleek space looks like it belongs in Tokyo or New York with its recessed, soft lighting and spare wood tables. The menu changes according to the daily fish delivery, and most preparations are raw (sashimi, sushi, carpaccio). Cooked dishes include steamed and grilled variations on the same. **$$**

 F5 VIA DELLA PENITENZA 7
06-68-30-70-53

AUGUSTO

At rough-and-tumble Augusto, traditional Roman food, like pasta with lentils, is dished out from pot to plate right in front of you. You might have to order in the kitchen or share a table with strangers at this exuberantly noisy place, but you'll leave well fed for less than $10 a person. **$**

 A3 PIAZZA DEI RENZI 15
06-58-03-798

BABINGTON'S TEA ROOM

 An elegant place to get a spot o' tea, Babington's also serves pancakes and bacon until 11 A.M. Tea service is formal and on the expensive side, but an hour here, away from the noise of the nearby Spanish Steps, is a grounding experience. **$$**

 D4 PIAZZA DI SPAGNA 23
06-67-86-027

▲

IL BACARO

An intimate, informal space on a tiny piazza near the Pantheon, Il Bacaro serves light meals – salads, sandwiches, and a hot dish or two – but the real draw is its rotating list of 25 wines by the glass, all well priced and among the best in their respective regions. **$**

 A9 VIA DEGLI SPAGNOLI 27
06-68-64-110

BAR GIANICOLO

A real neighborhood bar open until 1 A.M., the Gianicolo is a tiny place with an energetic aura. It's also one of the few places in Rome where you can get fresh carrot juice, even with a dash apple, celery, or beet thrown in for good measure. **$**

 B1 PIAZZALE AURELIO 5
06-58-06-275

IL BICCHIERE DI MASTAI

Chef-owner Fabio Baldassarre worked in Heinz Beck's La Pergola before opening this small, gracious wine bar. The menu, while small, is sophisticated, born of seasonal ingredients. You might find grilled sea bass or an elegant antipasto of buffalo milk mozzarella, smoked salmon, and roasted peppers with *crostini*. **$$**

 C3 VIA DEI BANCHI NUOVI 52
06-68-19-22-28

IL BRILLO PARLANTE

The best place for a snack or light meal near Piazza del Popolo, this wine bar and café pours 20 wines by the glass and serves salads, pastas, and grilled meats in inviting wood-paneled rooms. **$**

 C2 VIA DELLA FONTANELLA 12
06-32-43-334

CAFFÈ FARNESE

Just around the bend from Campo dei Fiori with a view of the Ghetto's main drag, Caffè Farnese is a great place to while away the hours over coffee by day and cocktails by night. The food, mainly sandwiches and salads, is secondary to the experience. **$**

 C2 VIA DEI BAULLARI 186
06-68-80-21-25

CAFFÈ PARNASSO

This chic Parioli haunt has some of the best pastries in town. Sandwiches, soups, and salads are also available for takeout or a sit-down meal throughout the day. **$**
OFF MAP PIAZZA DELLE MUSE 22
06-80-79-741

CAFFÈ SANT'EUSTACHIO

One of the two most famous cafés in Rome, this Roman coffee institution will add sugar to your espresso unless you say otherwise. The house-roasted beans are superb, and the service is lightning fast. $

 D9 PIAZZA SANT'EUSTACHIO 82
06-68-61-309

CAMPO

A sweet little spot for some of the better Chinese food in the city, Campo draws a big crowd of shoppers during lunch. At night, the place is more subdued, and the waiters have time to talk about the menu, which has a healthy, MSG-less slant. $$

 B2 PIAZZA DELLA CANCELLERIA 64
06-68-30-11-62

IL CANTINIERE DI SANTA DOROTEA

Open until 2 A.M. (late by Roman standards), this welcoming cantina serves 35 wines by the glass in all price ranges. The menu always features at least one soup and a variety of *salumi* and salads. The service is swift, but you are free to linger longer. $

 A3 VIA DI SANTA DOROTEA 9
06-58-19-025

CAVALIERI HILTON

Presented in elegant buffet style, the most lavish brunch in Rome is served at this grand hotel on the hill. Tuxedoed servers bring delectables like sushi, omelettes, and carved meats, and the views of the city are stunning on a clear day. $$$

OFF MAP VIA CADLOLO 101
06-35-091

CAVOUR 313

One of Rome's first wine bars, Cavour is a homey spot for a pre-dinner date or a light snack. Here you can always find the perfect cheese or salad to accompany your choice of the 25 wines available by the glass. $

 C3 VIA CAVOUR 313
06-67-85-496

CHECCHINO DAL 1887

Serious Roman cooking can be found in this Monte Testaccio perch. *Pajate* (intestines), *zampette* (pig's feet), and *coratella* (heart of beef) are all standard menu items, but there's also pasta and more common meat dishes, like stewed lamb, for the less adventurous. $$$

OVERVIEW MAP F3 VIA DI MONTE TESTACCIO 30 • 06-57-46-318

IL CHICCO D'UVA

Because it's next door to the Senate, this upscale dining room is popular among politicos who work late. Elegant and invariably rich dishes, such as goose carpaccio, homemade pastas with lots of cream, and all manner of veal, are served with big wines to match. Dinner only. $$

 B8 CORSO DEL RINASCIMENTO 70
06-68-67-983

IL CONVIVIO

Locals laud this open, airy restaurant for its surprising, eclectic menu. The owners hail from the Marches region, so the fish is first-rate. Other notable dishes venture into un-Italian combinations like pork with prunes or stuffed pheasant with raspberry confit. $$

 A7 VICOLO DEI SOLDATI 31
06-68-69-432

CUL DE SAC

A well-priced international wine list, along with very good food – like vegetable tarts, *insalatoni* (main course salads), and homemade desserts – make this ultracasual spot near Piazza Navona a favorite among locals and visitors alike. Only a lucky few will be able to snag one of the coveted outside tables. $

 D7 PIAZZA DI PASQUINO 73
06-68-80-10-94

DA BAFFETTO

One of the top pizzerias in town, this large restaurant does a fast turnover in traditional Roman pizza (i.e., thin crust), with standard toppings like mozzarella and tomatoes with basil.

The outdoor tables are most popular, but the simple inside space is elbow-to-elbow as well. $

 C5 VIA DEL GOVERNO VECCHIO 114
06-68-61-617

▲

DA CHECCO ER CARRETTIERE

With braids of garlic hanging over the tables and the nonlocal clientele, Da Checco may look like many Italian restaurants in the States, but it is one of the best traditional restaurants in Rome. Don't miss the *bucatini all'amatriciana,* hollow spaghetti with a tomato, pancetta, and onion sauce. $$

 A3 VIA BENEDETTA 10
06-58-17-018

DA GIGGETTO

This torchbearer for Jewish-Italian cooking serves loyal regulars who dine on fried zucchini flowers in season and *baccalà* (salt cod) and artichokes (prepared *alla giudea* – flattened and pan-fried) year-round. If you come in a second time, servers will remember and ask your name. $$

 E6 VIA DEL PORTICO D'OTTAVIA 21A
06-68-61-105

DAL TOSCANO

Most of the tables in this cozy, family-run Tuscan restaurant are in view of the wood-fired grill, upon which beef, lamb, and sausages are cooked to perfection. The classic *ribollita* (day-old soup served with bread in the bottom of the bowl) is a winter treat. $$

 A3 VIA GERMANICO 58
06-39-72-57-17

DA LUCIA

A meal at this friendly family operation will leave you full for days. The menu changes at the whim of the chef, but always includes hearty Roman dishes like spaghetti *alla gri-*

cia (with bacon, cracked pepper, and a generous serving of pecorino). The décor here is simple, with wooden tables, soft lighting, and a private patio. $$

 A3 VICOLO DEL MATTONATO 2
06-58-03-601

DAR POETA

Everyone has a favorite *pizzaiolo* (pizza maker) in Rome, and many seem partial to Dar Poeta. The secret? The flour used here is said to be easier to digest. Regardless of the scientifics, their concoctions – especially the margherita – taste great. $

 A3 VICOLO DEL BOLOGNA 45
06-58-80-516

LA DITA E LA LUNA

The caponata at this superlative Sicilian restaurant is worth the trip across town to San Lorenzo. The other offerings include an untraditional menu and an unbelievably well-priced wine list. The atmosphere, with the lights turned low, invites intimacy. $$

 F6 VIA DEI SABELLI 51
06-49-40-726

DITIRAMBO

 A cross between a casual trattoria and an experimental, chef-driven restaurant, this small dining room with bare wooden tables and fresh flowers emphasizes market-fresh, often organic ingredients. Its location just around the corner from Campo dei Fiori means lots of just-picked seasonal vegetables. $$

 B2 PIAZZA DELLA CANCELLERIA 74
06-68-71-626

EL TOULÀ

El Toulà is an elegant bastion of hospitality, where service is as important as food. The restaurant is a Roman institution, as are its signature dishes: *fegato alla veneziana* (sweet-and-sour liver) and *baccalà mantecato* (salt cod whipped with milk). Jacket and tie required for men. $$$

E2 VIA DELLA LUPA 29B
06-68-73-750

ENOTECA FERRARA

The offerings at this casual restaurant/wine bar change weekly and range from small snack-sized portions to full-on meals. Servers are well versed in the encyclopedic wine list, which has selections from every region in Italy, and make you feel right at home. $$

 A3 VIA DEL MORO 1A
06-58-03-769

EVANGELISTA

Said to be best in winter, Evangelista's destination dish is *carciofi al mattone* (artichokes roasted between two hot bricks). Simple pasta dishes, like linguine alla carbonara, are also adeptly prepared. Shoppers often stop in here after a day in nearby boutiques. $$

 E3 VIA DELLE ZOCCOLETTE 11A
06-68-75-810

FAGIANETTO

Don't be fooled by the menu *turistico* sign posted out front: This neighborhood favorite is delicious and inexpensive. You'll find hearty pastas with cream sauces and roasted meats, and everything, down to the tiramisu, is homemade. Despite the somewhat dicey Termini Station surrounds, the ambience is warm and inviting. $

 F3 VIA FILIPPO TURATI 21
06-44-67-306

FILETTI DI BACCALÀ

This Roman institution, somewhat of a dive, specializes in one thing and one thing only: greaselessly fried salt cod fillets, served with *puntarelle,* a local chicory, in winter. There are other things on the menu, but few people seem to notice. $

 C3 LARGO DEI LIBRARI 88
06-68-64-018

FORNO DI CAMPO DEI FIORI DI BARTOCCI E ROSCIOLI

 This small storefront, tucked near the Campo dei Fiori market, is the best place in the whole city for pizza *al taglio* (by the slice). All the pedestrian traffic moving in and out makes it easy to spot. Staff are always harried, but couldn't be friendlier. $

 C3 PIAZZA CAMPO DEI FIORI 22
06-68-80-66-62

IL GELATO DI SAN CRISPINO

 A favorite *gelateria* among favorites, San Crispino is so serious about its gelato that you aren't allowed to eat it in a cone, as the flavor might be compromised. Some of the unusual flavors featured here, like wild strawberry, have a season of less than a month. $

 F4 VIA DELLA PANETTERIA 42
06-67-93-924

GIOLITTI

Often on locals' short lists of best *gelaterie* in town, Giolitti offers its cold desserts in a selective number of mouthwatering seasonal flavors. The best are *nocciola* (hazelnut) and *fragola* (strawberry). $

 A10 VIA UFFICI DEL VICARIO 40
06-69-91-243

GRAPPOLO D'ORO

This restaurant's popularity among Americans surged after a *New Yorker* article called it a "classic trattoria," and a foreign clientele has dominated it ever since. The menu is traditional Roman, accented by lighter, fish-based specials that attract a fair share of local power-lunchers. $$

 B2 PIAZZA DELLA CANCELLERIA 80
06-68-97-080

'GUSTO

Occupying a lovely building with mostly bare white walls and distressed wood floors, this multiplex-like space is equal parts wine bar, pizzeria, restaurant, and culinary store. The upstairs eatery features a successful Asian-fusion menu. $$$

 D2 PIAZZA AUGUSTO IMPERATORE 7/9 •06-32-26-273

HAMASEI
Without a doubt the best Japanese restaurant in Rome, Hamasei is an oasis of calm in the middle of the buzzing Tridente. Waiters speak Japanese, Italian, and English, and the menu, as well as the service, is traditional Japanese. $$

 E4 VIA DELLA MERCEDE 35
06-67-92-134

HOTEL DE RUSSIE
The food at the garden courtyard inside this luxurious hotel might make you wonder if you're really in Rome: Traditional English and American breakfasts are available, as are bran muffins and smoothies. Italian *cornetti* (croissants) are an option for when-in-Rome adherents. $$

 B2 VIA DEL BABUINO 9
06-32-88-81

HOTEL D'INGHILTERRA
Wake up to elegance at this bastion of 19th-century gentility. English breakfasts are the standard fare, but variations on this theme – like scrambled eggs – are also offered on request. There's a pastry tray for those interested in a small meal, as well as a good tea selection. $$

 D3 VIA BOCCA DI LEONE 14
06-69-981

L'EAU VIVE
Arguably the strangest dining experi-. ence in Rome, this restaurant is run by nuns who sing between courses and invite you to join them. The food is classic French, with the likes of steak *frites* and roast pigeon dotting the menu. All profits are donated to charity. $$

 A5 VIA MONTERONE 85
06-68-80-10-95

LE SANS SOUCI
Le Sans Souci hosts see-and-be-seen diners in its elegant banquettes and serves a fusion of French and Italian classics, prepared in the heavier French style. Desserts, especially the chocolate soufflé, are over the top. $$$

 B1 VIA SICILIA 20
06-42-01-25-58

MACCHERONI
With its casual trattoria ambience and contemporary décor, this boisterous place caters to a young, attractive, and mostly local crowd. Dishes are of the traditional Roman variety, and standouts include penne *all'arrabi-ata*, which can be as spicy as you want it. $

 A9 PIAZZA DELLE COPPELLE 44
06-68-30-78-95

MIRÒ
This Banchi Nuovi spot serves up southern Italian food with heat. The focus here is on Calabrian cuisine, and the menu offers staples like rigatoni calabresi (with broccoli and sausage) and eggplant and dried tomatoes with oil and hot peppers. $$

 B3 VIA DEI BANCHI NUOVI 8
06-68-80-85-27

▲

MONTE CARUSO
Southern Italian food takes center stage in this stucco-arched, terra cotta-floored space. The stuffed pasta dishes – like the rigatoni and cannelloni – are as good as a trip to Basilicata or Calabria, and the service could not be more gracious. $$

 F2 VIA FARINI 12
06-48-35-49

MYOSOTIS
One of Rome's first restaurants to explore *cucina nuova*, Myosotis now has a strong hold on locals and tourists alike with its near-Pantheon address and perennially inventive food. Handmade pasta and fish are always good choices, and the desserts are refreshingly light, almost healthy. $$

 A9 VICOLO DELLA VACCARELLA 3
06-68-65-554

NEL REGNO DI RE FERDINANDO II
A Neapolitan restaurant through and through, this hot spot is named for a king, and you can expect to eat like one. This is a wonderful place to try

mozzarella di bufala in antipasto or pasta courses. Pastries are imported daily from Naples and are a welcome change from Roman sweets. **$$**
OVERVIEW MAP F3 VIA DI MONTE TESTACCIO 39 •06-57-83-725

NINO
Nino, with its wood-paneled walls, is a quiet restaurant even when it's full of Via Condotti shoppers. The menu features very simple, satisfying food, such as homemade *papardelle* with rabbit sauce and grilled vegetables with aged balsamic vinegar. **$$**

 E4 VIA BORGOGNONA 11 06-67-86-752

NON SOLO PIZZA
The main business here is pizza by the slice, but there's also pasta and salads for those looking for something more substantial. Take your food to go, or dine in the no-frills space with a made-to-order meal. **$**

 A3 VIA DEGLI SCIPIONI 95 06-37-25-820

▲

OMBRE ROSSE
Popular with Pasquino theatergoers, Ombre Rosse packs most of its tables outside on a small piazza that extends out from the kitchen. Main course salads, as well as sandwiches and cheese plates, are on offer, along with inexpensive wines by the glass. **$$**

 A3 PIAZZA SANT'EGIDIO 12 06-58-84-155

OSTERIA AI MERCATI
A popular southern Testaccio reservation, Ai Mercati always has a *bruschetta* of the day for its clientele of locals in the mood for traditional food. Main courses feature fresh pastas, grilled and roasted meats, and homemade desserts. Some of the after-dinner liqueurs are also homemade. **$**
OVERVIEW MAP F3 PIAZZA DEL GAZOMETRO 1 •06-57-43-091

OSTERIA DELL'INGEGNO
The décor is contemporary, and the ambience is decidedly upscale, belying the informality that the term "osteria" brings to mind. But the menu fits the bill with excellent daily choices, such as sweet and sour duck and ravioli with goat cheese. **$$**

 B12 PIAZZA DI PIETRA 45 06-67-80-662

OSTERIA DEL PESCE
This sleek, techno space offers a marine-based menu. The choices might include *polpette* (meatballs) made from *baccalà* rather than meat or *involtini* (rolls) of smoked salmon. **$$**

 B1 VIA MONSERRATO 32 06-68-65-617

OSTRICHE A COLAZIONE
The restaurant's name literally means "oysters for breakfast," even though it's only open for dinner. The loyal clientele of discriminating fish lovers enjoys a tartare of the day or simple cooked preparations of lobster, shrimp, and Mediterranean fish in this elegant, candlelit setting. **$$**

 B5 VIA DEI VASCELLARI 21 06-58-98-896

OTELLO ALLA CONCORDIA
Even though it's on a major shopping street, this friendly spot draws plenty of local businesspeople who want to dine *fuori* (outdoors) at lunch and dinner. The menu specializes in Roman and other central Italian regional dishes. **$$**

 D3 VIA DELLA CROCE 81 06-67-91-178

PANATTONI
The noise can be deafening and the service brusque, but Panattoni serves one of the finest, thinnest-crusted pizzas that this city offers. You can watch the preparation take place from start to finish on the marble slabs responsible for the pizzeria's common nickname, "L'Obitorio" (The Morgue). **$**

 C4 VIALE TRASTEVERE 53 06-58-00-919

PAPÀ BACCUS
A simultaneously upmarket and homey Tuscan restaurant just off Via

Veneto, Papà Baccus grills its famous *bistecche fiorentine* (T-bone steak) and serves it simply with olive oil and salt. Wonderful side dishes might include chicories with fava beans, arugula and tomato salad, or roasted potatoes. $$$

 B1 VIA TOSCANA 36
06-42-74-28-08

PARIS

Choose a fish from a rolling silver cart packed with ice, and have it deboned and served family style by expert waiters. The fish here is so fresh that it won't even need a squeeze of lemon for flavor. For diners more inclined to turf than surf, classic Roman dishes also appear on the menu. $$$

 B3 PIAZZA SAN CALISTO 7A
06-58-15-378

PASSETTO

With its filled courtyard out back and its proximity to Piazza Navona, this popular restaurant hosts a lively crowd. The food is traditional Roman, and the grilled baby lamb is a treat in springtime. $$

 A7 VIA ZANARDELLI 14
06-68-80-36-96

LA PENNA D'OCA

The Sardinian restaurateur's love of fish is evident in his inspired menu of *aragosta* (lobster), roasted *sarago* fish, and homemade pastas with the day's shellfish catch. He also creates a casual, familiar atmosphere, often greeting patrons, who include Roman regulars and well-heeled tourists, at the door himself. $$

 C2 VIA DELLA PENNA 53
06-32-02-898

LA PERGOLA

Heinz Beck's restaurant at the Cavalieri Hilton is still Rome's top culinary destination. Small, exquisite dishes with an eye toward presentation come with a gorgeous view of the Eternal City. The international, Mediterranean-influenced menu offers surprisingly little pasta. $$$

OFF MAP VIA CADLOLO 101
06-35-09-22-11

PERILLI

Come admire Perilli's décor, which hasn't changed for almost a hundred years. The trattoria atmosphere here is convivial, and the menu makes only the occasional nod to the changing seasons – most dishes are made from year-round staples like *pajata* (intestines), dried pastas, and root vegetables. $

 **F6** VIA MARMORATA 39
06-57-42-415

PIERLUIGI

A table in this longtime haunt for ex-pats and Italians in the film industry can be hard to come by. The food – mostly simply prepared pastas, meats, and fish – is served in a beautiful outdoor setting, but when the weather gets cold, the party moves inside to the cozy, low-ceilinged dining room. $$

 E6 PIAZZA DEI RICCI 144
06-68-61-302

PIPERNO

Sunday brunch is the only early meal served here, but it's a must on any vacation itinerary. Otherwise, traditional Jewish dishes, like fried zucchini flowers, *baccalà*, and artichokes, are brought out by a waitstaff of old-timers in sizes that the whole table can share. Outdoor seating in the small piazza is delightful. $$

 E5 VIA MONTE DEI CENCI 9
06-68-80-66-29

REEF

Sporting wood floors with inlaid glass, this nautical-chic hot spot serves both raw and cooked fish, as well as a few traditional pasta dishes like *cacio e pepe*. $$$

 D2 PIAZZA AUGUSTO
IMPERATORE 42 •06-68-30-14-30

RIPARTÉ CAFE

An open space with modern art on the walls, this place fills up at night with *trasteverini* and other Romans looking to try the selective, Italian-fusion menu. Fish is its strong suit, and sea bass and salmon are often the highlights. **$$**

 D3 VIA DEGLI ORTI DI TRASTEVERE 1 •06-58-611

RISTORANTE DAL BOLOGNESE
Despite its location on Piazza del Popolo, the busy Ristorante dal Bolognese caters to politicos more than shoppers. The food, straightforward traditional cuisine from Bologna, is less important than being seen at one of the packed outdoor tables. **$$**

 B2 PIAZZA DEL POPOLO 1 06-36-11-426

ROMAN GARDEN LOUNGE
Homemade ravioli, fresh fish, and seasonal vegetables prepared in various Mediterranean styles are at the forefront of Hotel d'Inghilterra's restaurant. Most diners come laden with shopping bags and use the elegant yet noisy space to refresh and refuel. **$$$**

 D3 VIA BOCCA DI LEONE 14 06-69-98-11

ROSATI
An old left-wing haunt, Rosati is where Antonio Gramsci et al. used to hang out. Today it sees more day-trippers from the nearby shopping areas nibbling on its reliable salads, soups, and sandwiches. Most of the seating is outside, right on Piazza del Popolo. **$**

 B2 PIAZZA DEL POPOLO 5 06-32-25-859

LA ROSETTA
Many consider this elegant, wood-paneled restaurant the best for fish in the entire city. All-fish tasting menus are the best way to experience the kitchen's range, which spans simple grilled catch to light pastas with shellfish. All are delicious and unimaginably fresh. **$$$**

 B10 VIA ROSETTA 9 06-68-61-002

SANGALLO
 Primarily a seafood restaurant, Sangallo offers tasting menus that are a fabulous value given the qual-ity of ingredients; the sea bass baked in a sea salt crust is otherworldly. The tiny space, with its discreet servers, candlelight, and fresh-cut flowers, is perfect for a second date. **$$**

 A9 VICOLO DELLA VACCARELLA 11A 06-68-65-549

SANTA LUCIA
Almost all seats here are outdoors under mature trees decorated with lights. The food is equally creative, light, and mostly healthy, and small courses are offered for those who don't want a huge meal. Santa Lucia also specializes in fish dishes from the Amalfi Coast. **$$**

 B7 LARGO FEBO 12 06-68-80-24-27

SAN TEODORO
One of the few quality restaurants near the Colosseum, San Teodoro is famous for its *carciofi alla giudea* (fried baby artichokes). Other nicely prepared dishes include homemade ravioli and a fresh fish of the day. Try to sit in the fabulous, bustling patio. **$$**

 D1 VIA DEI FIENILI 50 06-67-80-933

SETTIMIO ALL'ARANCIO
Proof that a homey restaurant can also be sophisticated, this family-run eatery serves Italian comfort food extraordinaire, including some of the city's best risotto, with zucchini flowers and pecorino, and the waitstaff has an age-old quality. **$$**

 E2 VIA DELL'ARANCIO 50 06-68-76-119

SHAKI
Though a bit overpriced, Shaki is nonetheless a good stop for a healthy lunch near the Via Condotti. There are fresh squeezed juices, sandwiches, and *insalatoni* (main course salads), served in a tranquil interior space or outside on the fairly quiet side street. **$$**

 D3 VIA MARIO DEI FIORI 29A 06-67-89-244

IL SIMPOSIO DI CONSTANTINI
This upscale wine bar is the perfect place to rest after a day at the Vatican Museums. From the sophisticated menu, try the house-smoked

fish assortment or a cheese course, served with fresh or dried fruit. Afterwards, take home a bottle from its wine store next door. $

 B6 PIAZZA CAVOUR 16
06-32-11-502

LA SOFFITTA

If you favor Neapolitan pizza, with a thicker, but still crisp crust, over Roman, look no further than La Soffitta, an out-of-the-way pizzeria that's worth a commute; the cheeseless margherita is the purest culinary incarnation of Naples to be found. The space itself is no-frills, as is the friendly service. $$

 B5 VIA DEI VILLINI 1
06-44-04-642

SORA LELLA

The menu at this Isola Tiberina eatery may change daily, but the homey atmosphere, with traditional Roman food to match, is a dependable constant. The worn in wood-paneled rooms look like they could tell some fascinating stories, if their walls could talk. $$

 F6 VIA PONTE QUATTRO CAPI 16
06-68-61-601

TAZZA D'ORO

The coffeehouse that competes with Caffè Sant'Eustachio for the title Best in Rome, Tazza d'Oro has round-the-clock bean roasters and a sales area for take-home business. Serious coffee drinkers down espresso standing up at the bar, and neighborhood regulars pop in several times a day. $

 B10 VIA D'ORFANI 84
06-67-89-792

LA TERRAZZA DELL'EDEN

With commanding views of Rome, La Terrazza allows diners to relax for hours within candlelit, white-tableclothed elegance. Dishes like a grapefruit, lobster, and baby zucchini appetizer and an oven-baked turbot with lemon and capers characterize the simply designed choices. $$$

 D5 VIA LUDOVISI 49
06-47-81-21

TESTA

Suburbia goes chic with this wine bar that doubles as a restaurant. The focus is on top-quality regional ingredients, like San Daniele prosciutto and Ligurian olives, and the chef will spare no expense to acquire them. Testa is a wholly artisanal venture, right down to the wines that are perfect for each menu item. $

OVERVIEW MAP A5 VIA TIRSO 30
06-85-30-06-92

TRAM TRAM

Named for its location along the tram route into the neighborhood, this place is no-frills, noisy, and seriously good. Sit down at one of the wooden tables and savor a dish like fava beans with chicories, simple roast chicken, or fried fresh anchovies, all served alongside a small and inexpensive wine list. $$

 F7 VIA DEI RETI 44
06-49-04-16

TRATTORIA

This is as simple as home-style Italian food ever gets. The *bucatini all'amatriciana* is very Roman, though the restaurant itself – with wooden tables and no menu – seems like it could be in the Lazio countryside. Reservations are not accepted. $

 F2 VIA DEI PREFETTI 19
06-68-73-752

TRATTORIA MONTI

The Camerucci family runs this friendly place that is a short walk from the Colosseum. The most famous white wine from the owners' home region of the Marches, Verdicchio, is served along with all manner of soups, stews, and fish dishes. $$

 B5 VIA DI SAN VITO 13
06-44-66-573

TRIMANI WINE BAR

Run by the folks who own the food shop of the same name, this *enoteca* opens at 11:30 A.M. The kitchen turns out only a couple of dishes, but they're all well-prepared. There are at least 15 wines by the glass, but if that's not enough, the shop conducts tastings and classes. $

 C3 VIA CERNAIA 37B
06-44-69-630

VALZANI

 A great Roman pastry shop with seasonal offerings, Valzani will always have staples like tiramisu and zabaglione cake. Just going in is an experience: everyone seems like a regular customer – and probably is. $

 A4 VIA DEL MORO 37B
06-58-03-792

VECCHIA LOCANDA

This restaurant has been going strong for nearly 75 years, thanks to its location near Torre Argentina and its faithfulness to Roman culinary tradition – you won't find a better bowl of *bucatini all'amatriciana*. The peaceful, candlelit room seems a world away from the city outside. $$

 B5 VICOLO SINIBALDI 2
06-68-80-28-31

▲

LA VERANDA DEL'HOTEL COLUMBUS

The city's most stunning outdoor restaurant – with tiki torches and big, mature trees – features *cucina nuova*, light versions of Italian classics. Servers are unobtrusive and efficient so that nothing gets in the way of a romantic evening. $$$

 C5 BORGO SANTO SPIRITO 73
06-68-72-973

▲

VINERIA

This quintessential Roman wine bar in Campo dei Fiori is a see-and-be-seen spot. The drink menu is fun, the bartenders give generous pours, and securing a table outside makes you feel like all is right with the world, if only for an hour. $

 C3 CAMPO DEI FIORI 15
06-68-80-32-68

WINE TIME

At this wine shop/café, snacks and heartier meals are served on spare wood tables for two, although the waitstaff will happily move the furniture around to accommodate larger parties. Wine Time is one of the few eateries in Rome that accepts reservations. $$

 A2 PIAZZA PASQUALE PAOLI 15
06-68-75-706

ZI' FENIZIA

Named after the owner's Aunt Fenizia, this is the only place in Rome to get kosher pizza. The delicious house specialty, *aciughe e indivia* (anchovies and endive), and 39 other flavors are doled out by the meter. Most people take it to go, but some stay and stand in the ever-bustling shop. $

 D5 VIA SANTA MARIA DEL
PIANTO 64 •06-68-96-976

DIRECTORY OF SHOPS

AI MONASTERI

Cistercian monks from various Italian monasteries make by hand all the products sold here. Gourmets revere the liqueurs, jams, chocolates, and other foodstuffs from this central shop.

 B8 CORSO RINASCIMENTO 72 06-68-80-27-83

ALINARI

Original black-and-white photographs of Italian cities taken by members of the Alinari family are the focus here. The Alinaris have run this shop since the 1800s and have an eye for urban life.

 D3 VIA ALIBERT 16A 06-67-92-923

AMORE E PSICHE

Specializing in psychology, arts, and humanities books, this small but densely packed store also stocks a good selection of classics in English.

 A6 VIA DI SANTA CATERINA DA SIENA 61 •06-67-83-908

▲

ANGLO-AMERICAN BOOK CO.

A well-regarded business among expats, Anglo-American carries U.S. and British titles and specializes in fiction and nonfiction.

 E4 VIA DELLA VITE 102 06-67-95-222

ANTICA ERBORISTERIA

 Featuring both prepackaged and made-to-order herbal remedies, the quaint Antica Erboristeria also sells antique pharmaceutical supplies, handmade paper, and licorice. Shopkeepers are all trained herbalists.

 B5 VIA DI TORRE ARGENTINA 15 06-68-79-493

ART DECO GALLERY

An eclectic collection of original French, Italian, and Austrian home accessories from the 1920s and '30s, this gallery sells mostly furniture, vases, and lighting.

 B6 VIA DEI CORONARI 14 06-67-86-241

ARTE

Form and function unite at this beautiful showcase of contemporary design. Everything – from blenders to dish racks – is assessed for quality as well as aesthetic beauty.

 B9 PIAZZA RONDANINI 32 06-68-33-907

AVC BY ADRIANA CAMPANILE

 Classic Italian shoes and handbags are the only things on the menu at this lovely boutique responsible for outfitting Romans and visitors of all levels of fame.

 D4 PIAZZA DI SPAGNA 88/89 06-67-80-095

AVEDA DAY SPA

This Roman outpost of the American spa chain occupies a beautiful location adjacent to the Spanish Steps and offers a full suite of natural skin, hair, nail, and massage services.

 D4 RAMPA MIGNANELLI 9 06-69-92-42-57

BACO DA SETA

Elegant day- and eveningwear for women drape the racks of this high-quality silk merchant. Patrons will also have the benefit of the staff's expert eye for fitting.

 D3 VIA VITTORIA 75 06-67-93-907

BATTISTONI

 A well-established men and women's clothing store, Battistoni designs its own suits, shirts, shoes, and accessories. Politicians like the conservative, sophisticated styles, and the Via Condotti address ensures quality.

E3 VIA CONDOTTI 60 06-67-86-827

BERTÉ

Berté is the grandest toy store in the city. Its display window, which often showcases doll collections or adorable stuffed animals, is a delightful distraction for the many strollers on ever-crowded Piazza Navona.

 C7 PIAZZA NAVONA 108
06-68-75-011

BEST SELLER
At this store off the main shopper's track near Campo dei Fiori, you'll find prêt-a-porter lines from all the famous designers, including Dolce & Gabbana, at great prices.

 C3 VIA DEI GIUBBONARI 96
68-13-60-40

BIBLI
The café here is as big a draw as the books, which include a large selection of novels in English. There's also a stage for live musical performances and computers for web surfing.

 B4 VIA DEI FIENAROLI 28
06-58-84-097

BRIGHENTI
 Located just off the Via Corso, Brighenti is a beautiful, dimly lit store that specializes in elegant silk lingerie. Bathing suits in interesting designs are also on offer.

 E4 VIA FRATTINA 7
06-67-91-484

BUCONE
Part candy store, part wine shop, and part café, Bucone has been in business for more than a century. The staff will take time and care with each order, and even the smallest purchase is presented with style.

 C2 VIA DI RIPETTA 19
06-36-12-514

BULGARI
 You'll have to ring before gaining entrance into the opulent world of Bulgari, a name syn-

onymous with exclusive jewelry designs. The store doesn't post regular hours, but someone is always inside during the normal business day.

 D4 VIA CONDOTTI 10
06-69-62-61

IL CANESTRO
This Testaccio institution draws health foodies from all over town and beyond with its organic foods, vitamin and herb supplements, and books on alternative medicine.

 F5 VIA LUCA DELLA ROBBIA 12
06-57-46-287

CARLO GIUNTA
This well-designed shop displays its wares sparingly. You'll find antique ceramic objects from all over Italy and contemporary Sicilian tableware known for its bright, playful colors.

 B4 VIA DEI CORONARI 83/84
06-68-64-192

CASTRONI
Homesick American tourists craving peanut butter and Rice Krispies can come here for a fix. Castroni also sells international cooking ingredients from China, Japan, Korea, and many Mediterranean countries.

 A5 VIA COLA DI RIENZO 196
06-68-74-383

LA CICOGNA
A one-stop shopping store for clothing and accessories for infants and children up to age 14, La Cicogna is a national chain with a lenient return and exchange policy and a satisfaction guarantee.

 E3 VIA FRATTINA 138
06-67-91-912

CINQUE LUNE
This tiny shop bakes some of the best cakes in Rome and also specializes in traditional seasonal pastries for Easter and Christmas, like panettone and pandora cakes.

 B8 CORSO DEL RINASCIMENTO 89
06-68-80-10-05

LA CITTÀ DEL SOLE
Densely packed and hard to navigate, this very politically correct store specializes in educational toys for children. Luckily, the staff knows where everything is

and will help you find what you're looking for.

 A9 VIA DELLA SCROFA 65
06-68-80-38-05

CONFETTERIA MORIONDO E GARIGLIO

A family operation, this chocolate maker specializes in holiday sweets – there's always a line out the door on Valentine's Day. The shop will also deliver to hotels within Rome.

 A7 VIA PIÈ DI MARMO 21/22
06-69-90-856

▲
CONSTANTINI

One of the best wine shops in the city, Constantini carries both everyday and collectible wines from all of Italy's 20 regions. The cellar master hand-selects each bottle.

 B6 PIAZZA CAVOUR 16
06-32-13-210

THE CORNER BOOK SHOP

 This tiny Trastevere bookseller stocks an amazing array of fiction and nonfiction, with many titles in English. Even the British imports, which are usually expensive, have reasonable price tags.

 A3 VIA DEL MORO 45
06-58-36-942

LA CORTE

This fishmonger deals in high-quality smoked piscatory products, like salmon and swordfish, and also stocks all manner of anchovies and sardines.

 B1 VIA DELLA GATTA 1
06-67-83-842

C.U.C.I.N.A.

The Italian version of Williams-Sonoma, this friendly store carries kitchen products of all kinds, from elaborate espresso makers to simple citrus zesters.

 D3 VIA MARIO DEI FIORI 65
06-67-91-275

DANIELA BILENCHI

Romans rely on Bilenchi to restore damaged porcelain and china, but the shop also sells antique lamps. Whether it's repaired or new to you, everything comes with a satisfaction guarantee.

 F2 VIA DELLA STELLETTA 17
06-68-75-222

DEGLI EFFETTI

This trio of boutiques divided by featured label is perhaps the most expensive clothing store outside the Piazza di Spagna area. You'll find the latest and hottest frocks from Japanese designers, as well as labels like Helmut Lang.

 B11 PIAZZA CAPRANICA 75, 79, 93
06-67-90-202

DOLCE & GABBANA

 Living up to its posh address, Dolce & Gabbana's sleek space showcases high fashion from the famous design team.

 D4 PIAZZA DI SPAGNA 94
06-69-38-08-70

DOLCEROMA

An unlikely combination of Viennese and American treats share space at this confectionery where traditional Austrian tortes and carrot cake sit alongside brownies and chocolate chip cookies.

 E6 VIA DEL PORTICO D'OTTAVIA 20B
06-68-92-196

DOROTEA

A new-age store in trendy Trastevere, Dorotea might be Rome's only purveyor of crystal magic and healing rocks. There's also a selection of bath and beauty products, including the house brand.

 C3 VIA ROMA LIBERA 11
06-58-80-497

THE ENGLISH BOOKSHOP

The concentration here, as the name implies, is English literature, as well as English translations of Italian works. This is an inevitable stop for anglophone travelers, and there's even a collection of eye-catching accessories.

 C2 VIA DI RIPETTA 248
06-32-03-301

ENOTECA VINICOLO ANGELINI

A fabulous selection of affordable vintages from Lazio, as well as pricey collectibles from all over the world, await the wine lover at this densely packed shop near Termini Station.

 A4 VIA VIMINALE 62
06-48-81-028

ENRICO CAMPONI

If you can't get to Venice, Enrico Camponi is *the* place in Rome to buy Murano glass. Many pieces, including some beautiful vases, are Venini antiques.

 F2 VIA DELLA STELLETTA 32
06-68-65-249

ESIA BOOKS AND JOURNALS

Popular with college students from La Sapienza, this bookshop carries the best English-language selection of academic texts in northern Rome, as well as a number of literary journals.

 D4 VIA PALESTRO 30
06-44-63-505

EVENTI

A place that's all about the '70s retro look, Eventi sells platform shoes and polyester outfits in psychedelic colors to the urban youth crowd.

 C2 VIA DELLA FONTANELLA 8
06-36-00-25-33

FARMACIA PESCI

In business since the 16th century, the oldest pharmacy in the Eternal City offers contemporary services (like prescription refills), as well as consultations on herbal and homeopathic remedies.

 F4 PIAZZA FONTANA DI TREVI 89
06-67-92-210

▲

FAUSTO SANTINI

This whimsical shoe and handbag designer has a loyal following of customers in the arts. His line changes from year to year, and the products are consistent in their cutting-edge quality.

 E3 VIA FRATTINA 120
06-67-84-114

FEDERICO BUCCELLATI

 This shop's display window, often showcasing ornate necklaces and large rings, is only a hint of what's inside. Specializing in fine silver pieces, Buccellati is also fond of tiaras, should you need one.

 E3 VIA CONDOTTI 31
06-67-90-329

FELTRINELLI INTERNATIONAL

 This outpost of the popular Italian bookstore carries Rome's best selection of English-language travel guides. Fiction and nonfiction titles, CDs, and DVDs in their original languages complete the global offerings.

 D2 VIA VITTORIO EMANUELE ORLANDO 84 •06-48-27-878

FEMME SISTINA

 Pamper yourself with a visit to this old-guard salon whose stylists have worked on celebrities like Audrey Hepburn and Nicole Kidman. Hair, skin, and nail services are all available in this spot next to Piazza di Spagna.

 D4 VIA SISTINA 75A
06-67-80-260

FOOD FOR THOUGHT

Located on the ground floor of the United Nations Building B, this shop sells English-language books, stationery, gift wrap, note cards, and area travel guides.

OVERVIEW MAP E4 VIA DELLE TERME DI CARACALLA B056 •06-57-29-73-00

FORNO DEL GHETTO

Devotees of this highly regarded traditional Jewish bakery line up outside on Sunday mornings, waiting to take home its fresh ricotta cake or pastries.

 E6 VIA DEL PORTICO D'OTTAVIA 1
06-68-78-637

FRANCESCO BIASIA

Among the most innovative handbag designers in the world, Biasia uses high-tech fabrics along with traditional animal skins to create functional purses of exceptional quality.

 E4 VIA DUE MACELLI 62
06-67-92-727

FRETTE

The world's most famous linen store, Frette – with its luxurious, elegant styles – is a thread-counter's dream. The sales in August, when everything but the retail stores is closed, cut prices up to 50 percent.

 F3 VIA DEL CORSO 381
06-67-86-862

GHERARDINI

Come here for the purchase that will carry home all your others. Gherardini designs bags with unique flair in sizes that range from small clutches to checked luggage.

 E3 VIA BELSIANA 48
06-67-95-501

GIOIELLI IN MOVIMENTO

Featuring items like rings with changeable stones, the unique jewelry designs here double as works of art, with prices to match. Custom designs are also an option for those who have something specific in mind.

 F2 VIA DELLA STELLETTA 22B
06-68-67-431

'GUSTO

A fun store with a slant toward international cooking, 'Gusto sells every imaginable kitchen accoutrement, like microplane zesters and high-tech espresso machines.

 D2 PIAZZA AUGUSTO IMPERA-
TORE 7/9 •06-32-36-363

▲

H. MARTINELLI

The Roman branch of this family-run mini-empire is the place to come for a once-in-a-lifetime purchase of art deco-influenced jewelry.

 D4 VIA MARIO DEI FIORI 59B
06-67-97-733

INNOCENZI

An international food store, Innocenzi carries imported products of all kinds, especially those from neighboring Mediterranean countries, such as Greek olive oil.

 C3 PIAZZA SAN COSIMATO 66
06-58-12-725

KOREAN MARKET

In addition to stocking nonperishable ingredients for Korean and other Asian recipes, this upscale store sells fresh snacks, small meals, and toothsome desserts. Prices are high, but so is the quality.

 B4 VIA CAVOUR 84
06-48-85-060

LAURA BIAGIOTTI

This large boutique sells original, fairly conservative suits, dresses, and separates for women and the sales consultants are all trained fitters. Feel free to browse – you won't get any pressure to buy.

 E3 VIA BORGOGNONA 43/44
06-67-91-205

LEONE LIMENTANI

This is *the* place in Italy to locate that missing piece of china. If you can't find it among this vast array of plates, cups, and bowls, there's a good chance it doesn't exist.

 E6 VIA DEL PORTICO D'OTTAVIA 47
06-68-80-69-49

LIBRERIA HERDER

The dense shelves of this friendly used bookstore – one of Rome's best – often yield obscure texts for the diligent browsers. The helpful staff is also happy to search for the titles you seek.

 A11 PIAZZA DI MONTECITORIO 117
06-67-94-628

LINN-SUI

In contrast to its traditional Roman surrounds, Linn-Sui is a big Japanese home store. Find Asian staples like lacquered furniture and sumptuous silks, as well as a good selection of futons.

 C4 VIA DEI BANCHI NUOVI 37
06-68-33-406

THE LION BOOKSHOP

With a stock of fiction and nonfiction titles in English, as well as a reading room and coffee and tea service, this cozy spot provides respite from the throngs of shoppers outside.

 D3 VIA DEI GRECI 33
06-32-65-40-07

LOCO

Always popular with the performing arts crowd, Loco is a funky, expensive shoe store on the cutting edge of design. Knowledgeable sales staff will personalize the service to find you the perfect fit.

 B3 VIA DEI BAULLARI 22
06-68-80-82-16

LUSH

Smelling almost good enough to eat, this shop – part of the British chain – spills over with handmade soaps, shampoos, lotions, potions, and tonics that are vegan-friendly and cruelty-free.

 C2 VIA DEI BAULLARI 112
06-68-30-18-10

MARIELA BURANI

This designer's Tridente shop showcases both her haute couture and her ready-to-wear designs. The choices in this small space range from loud and playful to more formal eveningwear.

 D3 VIA BOCCA DI LEONE 28
06-68-69-747

MARISA PADOVAN

Forget the chain lingerie stores along the Via Corso; Marisa Padovan is the only serious place to shop for quality swimsuits and intimate apparel, including custom-fitted bras.

 D3 VIA DELLE CARROZZE 81
06-67-00-630

MERCATO DI PORTA PORTESE

Rome's most famous flea market is also its largest, and there's no telling what you might find among the sprawl of vintage clothing, furniture, and home accessories that takes over Porta Portese every Sunday morning. Be sure to bargain.

 D4 PORTA PORTESE

MERCATO DELLA PIAZZA VITTORIO EMANUELE II

Housewives line up at this low-profile, boisterous outdoor food market near Termini Station for fresh breads, cheeses, vegetables, and even livestock.

 C6 PIAZZA VITTORIO EMANUELE II

IL MESSAGERIE

With two floors of international CDs, books, and DVDs, including a wide selection of Italian regional music, Il Messagerie is the best-stocked music store in the city.

 D3 VIA DEL CORSO 473
06-68-44-01

METAMORFOSI

For an urban retreat without the upmarket airs of the Via Condotti, head to this down-to-earth, value-oriented Testaccio day spa for a massage, wax, or coif.

 F4 VIA GIOVANNI BRANCA 94
06-57-47-576

MONDADORI

A well-stocked Vatican-area bookshop, Mondadori also sells CDs, DVDs, and literary gifts like reading accessories. Service is cordial, and some sales associates speak English.

 A6 PIAZZA COLA DI RIENZO 81
06-32-20-188

MONDELLO OTTICA

Mondello Ottica primarily focuses on designer eyewear, carrying both sunglasses and frames for prescriptions, and offers free adjustments and minor repairs.

 B2 VIA DEL PELLEGRINO 98
06-68-61-955

NARDECCHIA

Stop in this well-respected Piazza Navona gallery to admire its famous black-and-white prints of the city.

Prices to buy range from affordable to very expensive.

 C7 PIAZZA NAVONA 25
06-68-69-318

OFFICINA DELLA CARTA

This old-world custom stationer deals in handmade invitations, business cards, announcements, and the like. The staff will work with you to design your pieces and help navigate the range of aesthetic options.

 A3 VIA BENEDETTA 26B
06-58-95-557

ORNAMENTUM

The specialty of this beautiful fabric house – worth a visit just to gawk – is its luxurious silks for curtains and upholstery in every imaginable color. The store will also ship your purchases anywhere.

 B6 VIA DEI CORONARI 227
06-68-76-849

O TESTA

 This men's clothing store designs one-of-a-kind pieces and also hawks designer lines at a discount. Suits, in particular, are a bargain compared to other boutiques.

 E3 VIA FRATTINA 42/43
06-67-90-660

OTTICA EFFRATI

This Piazza di Spagna eyewear boutique presents all the big-name Italian designers, including Prada, Gucci, and Persol, along with the Japanese Kata line and trendy British brands.

 D4 PIAZZA DI SPAGNA 91
06-67-95-361

PANDORA

There's an odd assortment of gift items in this friendly Trastevere shop, from various inexpensive objects made of Murano glass to jewelry that could be described as shabby chic.

 B3 PIAZZA SANTA MARIA IN TRASTEVERE 6 •06-58-17-145

IL PAPIRO

 Find stationery for both everyday and extraordinary occasions at this pretty shop. Most of the papers are handmade, and there are calligraphy supplies as well.

 C10 VIA DEL PANTHEON 50
06-67-95-597

PINEIDER

Find the perfect gift for a recent college graduate or a new executive among Pineider's exclusive handmade Florentine leather desk accessories. Their custom services include invitations and engraving.

 E2 VIA DELLA FONTANELLA BORGHESE 22 •06-68-78-369

POLVERE DI TEMPO

A truly artisanal shop, Polvere di Tempo is a veritable studio for Adrian Rodriguez, who crafts hourglasses, sundials, and watches here. Stop by to see him working in the back room.

 A3 VIA DEL MORO 59
06-58-80-704

PROFUMERIA MATEROZZOLI

In business since 1870, this perfume store stocks all the major brands, plus some rare ones, like Acqua di Parma. For men, there are quality shaving accessories, too.

 E3 PIAZZA SAN LORENZO IN LUCINA 5 •06-68-89-26-86

QUADRIFOGLIO OUTLET

An upscale kids' boutique, Quadrifoglio concentrates on handmade infant and toddler clothing. Instead of having August sales, this shop keeps its prices low year-round.

 B10 VIA DELLE COLONELLE 10
06-67-84-917

RACHELE

Purveyor of the finest clothing for children, Rachele only carries handmade togs for infants to seven-year-olds. Special orders for older children (up to age 12) can be made upon request.

 B2 VICOLO DEL BOLLO 6
06-68-69-747

RICORDI

Stocking CDs from the world over, this large store keeps a particularly good selection of vintage Italian music from all 20 regions, especially Naples.

 B1 VIA CESARE BATTISTI 120
06-67-98-022

RINASCITA

Below the ground-floor bookstore that carries a few mainstream novels in English, Rinascita's basement holds its music collection of mostly new releases from Europe and the United States – a notable exception is the compelling selection of world music, especially from Latin America.

 C7 VIA DELLE BOTTEGHE OSCURE I •06-67-97-637

RIZZOLI

The Rome location of this sophisticated bookstore chain stocks art volumes by internationally acclaimed Italian painters and photographers, along with other bounties for the cultured reader.

F3 LARGO CHIGI 15
06-67-96-641

ROMA-STORE

This house of brand-name bath and beauty products changes its selection frequently, and what you see is what you get.

 B4 VIA DELLA LUNGARETTA 63
06-58-18-789

▲

SCALA QUATTORDICI

Scala Quattordici sells off-the-rack silk clothing for women, but also makes items to order in surprisingly little time. Among the accessories,

the richly colored scarves are excellent gifts.

 A3 VIA DELLA SCALA 13
06-58-83-580

▲

SERGIO VALENTE BEAUTY CENTER

Rome's upper crust has been patronizing this salon for years, but the staff will still treat new customers like family. Its signature services include customized facials and elaborate nail treatments.

 D4 VIA CONDOTTI 11
06-67-94-515

SERMONETA TIES

The cravat-savvy know Sermoneta for its variety, high quality, and reasonable prices. Don't be fooled by the name – the shop sells other accessories, like their fine line of leather gloves.

 D4 PIAZZA DI SPAGNA 61
06-67-91-960

SIMONA

Simona is a discreet lingerie shop for larger-than-average sizes. Here you can find high-quality, sexy, well-fitting bras, underwear, and sleepwear.

 D2 VIA DEL CORSO 83
06-36-00-18-36

LA SINOPIA

Antique experts staff this highly respected shop selling mostly furniture from the 18th and 19th centuries. They also consult on restoration and care of the valuable pieces you might acquire here.

 D3 VIA DEI BANCHI VECCHI 21C
06-68-72-869

I SOLITI IGNOTI

Specializing in gourmet foods from every region in Italy, I Soliti Ignoti stocks a tantalizing selection of edibles, including hard-to-find cheeses, wines, spices, and salamis. They also arrange, by appointment, on-site dinners for small groups.

 D6 VIA DEL TEATRO PACE 37
06-68-89-12-60

SPAZIO SETTE

A huge 17th-century palace houses this collection of mostly 20th- and 21st-century furniture. Don't worry about fitting your purchase on the plane – Spazio Sette will ship anywhere.

 C5 VIA DEI BARBIERI 7
06-68-69-747

STOCK MARKET

A home décor shop for those with global tastes, this large, eclectic emporium sells kitchen accessories, furniture, decorative throw pillows, and glassware.

 C3 VIA DEI BANCHI VECCHI 51
06-68-64-238

TANCA

Old photographic prints, heirloom jewelry, and estate silver are some of the disparate relics you'll find on offer at this cluttered, but very welcoming, shop.

 C9 SALITA DE CRESCENZI 12
06-68-75-272

TEBRO

As well-regarded locally as Frette is internationally, this sophisticated store sells high-quality linens, as well as elegant, understated lingerie.

 F2 VIA DEI PREFETTI 46
06-68-64-851

TOD'S

 This spare boutique gorgeously displays Tod's shoes and handbags that are famous for their quality leather in fabulous colors and classic styles.

 E3 VIA BORGOGNONA 45
06-67-86-828

TRIMANI

The shelves of this wine shop-cum-gourmet food store hold delicacies like truffle paste, dried porcini mushrooms, and exquisite olive oils that you can taste before you buy.

 C3 VIA GOITO 20
06-44-69-661

UPIM

If you've forgotten anything for your trip, stop by Upim for the unbelievably low prices on swimsuits, underwear, clothing, cosmetics, and toiletries.

 F3 VIA GIOBERTI 64
06-44-65-579

VALENTINO

This salon of haute couture is a mainstay of the area's upscale boutiques. Separate men's and women's shops showcase Valentino's penchant for the romantic and elegant.

 E3 VIA BOCCA DI LEONE 15
06-67-83-656

VICTORY

Victory carries well-priced Italian and French ready-to-wear lines geared toward the young nightclub crowd. For a preview of what the clothes look like on, check out the chic staff.

 C4 VIA SAN FRANCESCO A. RIPA 19
06-58-12-437

▲

VIOLA

This charcuterie's raison d'être is pork in its many guises. Among the choices are house-cured sausages, tender prosciutto, and fresh sausages that are perfect for grilling or adding to pasta dishes.

 C3 CAMPO DEI FIORI 43
06-68-80-61-14

VOLPETTI

Run by brothers Claudio and Emilio, Volpetti is without a doubt the best cheese store in Rome. Rinds of hand-selected, artisanal cheeses from all over Italy are lovingly washed each morning, and the products are shippable to anywhere in the world.

 F6 VIA MARMORATA 47
06-57-42-352

Ⓐ **AMUSEMENTS**

MUSEUMS AND GALLERIES

ASSOCIAZIONE CULTURALE L'ATTICO
The most avant-garde contemporary gallery in Rome, The Attic showcases young, mostly European artists. Many of the paintings, sculptures, and multimedia installations are implicitly political, and prices on pieces by up-and-comers are reasonable.

 B3 VIA DEL PARADISO 41
06-68-69-846

CAPPELLA SISTINA
See SIGHTS, p. 13.

 B2 VIALE VATICANO
06-69-88-38-60 OR
06-69-88-43-41

CASTEL SANT'ANGELO
See SIGHTS, p. 5.

 C5 LUNGOTEVERE CASTELLO 50
06-89-96-76-00

CATACOMBS
See SIGHTS, p. 6.

OFF MAP SAN CALLISTO: VIA APPIA ANTICA 110 • 06-51-30-15-80

OFF MAP SAN SEBASTIANO: VIA APPIA ANTICA 136 • 06-78-87-035

GALLERIA BORGHESE

This 17th-century villa holds one of the most important art collections in Rome. Permanent displays include sculptures by Bernini and paintings by Caravaggio, Raphael, and Rubens.

 A1 PIAZZA SCIPIONE BORGHESE 5
06-32-810

GALLERIA DELL'ACCADEMIA DI SAN LUCA
The collection of Accademia di San Luca, a private arts academy founded in the 1400s, includes Raphael's beloved painting *Madonna of St. Luke* and other Renaissance works.

 F4 PIAZZA DELL'ACCADEMIA DI SAN LUCA 77 • 06-67-89-243

GALLERIA DELLE CARTE GEOGRAFICHE
Pope Gregory XIII (of Gregorian calendar fame) designed this 394-foot-long gallery. You can view 16th-century maps of Italy from the observation point at the north end.

 B2 MUSEI VATICANI, VIALE VATICANO 06-69-88-38-60 OR 06-69-88-43-41

GALLERIA DORIA PAMPHILJ

The biggest attractions at this Pamphilj family compound are the three Caravaggio paintings, including *Rest on the Flight to Egypt.* The eclectic private collection also contains works by Titian and Guido Reni.

 B1 PIAZZA DEL COLLEGIO ROMANO 2 • 06-67-97-323

GALLERIA F. RUSSO
This gallery mounts shows by 20th-century Italian painters and photographers, such as Carlo Erba and De Chirico, with occasional exhibits of international work as well.

 D3 VIA ALIBERT 15A
06-67-89-949

▲

GALLERIA NAZIONALE D'ARTE ANTICA
Located in the Palazzo Barberini, this collection of paintings includes work by Raphael, Caravaggio, and Titian. Bernini contributed to the overall design of the dramatic building, including the grand staircase at the entrance.

 E6 VIA DELLE QUATTRO FONTANE 13 • 06-48-24-184

GALLERIA NAZIONALE D'ARTE MODERNA E CONTEMPORANEA
This gallery holds the nation's largest collection of modern Italian art. There's also a handful of pieces

by international painters, including Cezanne, Klimt, and Kandinsky.
OVERVIEW MAP A3 VIALE DELLE BELLE ARTI 131 •06-32-29-81

GALLERIA SPADA
Paintings by baroque artist Guido Reni comprise the contents of 16th-century Palazzo Spada. Don't miss the palace's interior garden with its trompe l'oeil fountain.

 D2 PIAZZA CAPO DI FERRO 3 06-68-74-896

MUSEI CAPITOLINI
See SIGHTS, p. 15.

 C1 INTERSECTION OF VIA DEL TEATRO DI MARCELLO, VIA DELLE TRE PILE, VIA DEL CAMPIDOGLIO, AND VIA SAN PIETRO IN CARLERE 06-67-10-20-71

MUSEI VATICANI
See SIGHTS, p. 13.

 B2 VIALE VATICANO 06-69-88-38-60 OR 06-69-88-43-41

MUSEO BARRACCO DI SCULTURA ANTICA
The pre-Roman sculptures assembled here include Babylonian stone lions, ancient Greek vases, and fragments of Greek carvings. All the pieces were part of baron Giovanni Barracco's private collection, which he donated to the city in the early 20th century.

 A3 CORSO VITTORIO EMANUELE II 168 •06-68-80-68-48

MUSEO D'ARTE EBRAICA
Located in the city's heavily guarded synagogue, this museum documents the legacy of Rome's Jewish population. Religious ritual objects, 16th-century papal decrees against the Jews, and personal effects from concentration camps are among the artifacts housed here.

 F6 LUNGOTEVERE DEI CENCI (SINAGOGA) 06-68-40-06-61

MUSEO D'ARTE ORIENTALE
Located near Santa Maria Maggiore, this little-touristed spot contains a well-organized display of ancient artifacts from the Near East, as well as finds from Tibet and China dating from the 11th to the 18th centuries.

 C5 VIA MERULANA 248 06-48-74-218

▲

MUSEO DEL CORSO
The rotating exhibitions at this privately owned and highly regarded museum tend to be small shows that detail the work and lives of internationally famous artists, writers, and historical figures.

 A1 VIA DEL CORSO 320 06-67-86-209

MUSEO DELLA MURA
The Museo della Mura delineates the construction of Rome's fortress against invaders in one of the most intriguing museum spaces in the city; it's housed in Porta San Sebastiano, the best-preserved ancient gate into the Eternal City.
OVERVIEW MAP F5 VIA DI PORTA SAN SEBASTIANO 18 •06 70 47 52 84

MUSEO DELLA VIA OSTIENSE
You'll find this little museum in an ancient gatehouse near the excavations at Ostia Antica. The exhibit traces the construction of the Ostian Way, which connected the city with the sea, in the 3rd century B.C.
OVERVIEW MAP F3 VIA R. PERSICHETTI 3 06-57-43-193

MUSEO DEL XXI SECOLO
This gargantuan space, still partially under construction, is Rome's premier museum for art shows of all media and genres and presents only 21st-century work.
OFF MAP VIA GUIDO RENI 10 06-32-02-438

MUSEO DI PALAZZO VENEZIA
This spectacular palazzo, which once housed Mussolini's offices, is now home to a sprawling and varied accumulation of Italian art, including one of the city's largest collections of porcelain and ceramics.

 B1 VIA DEL PLEBESCITO 118 06-69-99-43-19

MUSEO DI ROMA IN TRASTEVERE

 A quaint folklore collection in a 17th-century convent for Carmelite nuns, this small museum was renovated in 2000 to include temporary gallery space in the cloister.

 A3 PIAZZA SANT'EGIDIO 1B 06-58-16-563

MUSEO ETRUSCO DI VILLA GIULIA

Villa Giulia – the site of lavish summer parties in the 16th century – holds Italy's best collection of Etruscan art and artifacts under one roof. A visit here can last all day.

OVERVIEW MAP A3 PIAZZALE DI VILLA GIULIA 9 •06-32-26-571

MUSEO GREGORIANO EGIZIO

Part of the Vatican compound, this museum collects Egyptian art from 2,600 B.C. to 600 B.C. Hours vary widely, so call or check at the entrance to the Vatican Museums before visiting.

 B2 MUSEI VATICANI, VIALE VATICANO 06-69-88-38-60 OR 06-69-88-43-41

MUSEO GREGORIANO ETRUSCO

One of the most popular side museums of the Vatican collection, this extensive space contains Greek, Roman, and Etruscan works, including objects from the tomb of Regolini-Galassi, a well-preserved burial site from 650 B.C.

 B2 MUSEI VATICANI, VIALE VATICANO 06-69-88-38-60 OR 06-69-88-43-41

MUSEO GREGORIANO PROFANO

This museum of pagan antiquities includes extensive commentary about the Greek and Roman sculptures displayed.

 B2 MUSEI VATICANI, VIALE VATICANO 06-69-88-38-60 OR 06-69-88-43-41

MUSEO NAPOLEONICO

 The 16th-century Palazzo Primoli houses this small but dense array of Napoleonic artifacts.

 C6 PIAZZA PONTE UMBERTO I 1 06-68-80-62-86

MUSEO NAZIONALE DELLE PASTE ALIMENTARI

The guided tours at Rome's only museum devoted to food may provide too much information for the casual visitor, but cooks and food historians will appreciate the attention to minute detail.

 F4 PIAZZA SCANDERBERG 117 06-69-91-120

MUSEO NAZIONALE ROMANO – CRYPTA BALBI

Discovered in 1981, this archaeological expanse went on display in 2000. Its main attraction is the lobby of the ancient Teatro di Balbo, but interpretive space is used throughout the site to explain the practice of archaeology.

 C6 VIA DELLE BOTTEGHE OSCURE 31 •06-39-96-77-00

▲

MUSEO NAZIONALE ROMANO – PALAZZO ALTEMPS

The beautiful 15th-century palazzo is a wonderful place to pass an afternoon amidst intimate courtyards and ancient art, much of which was restored by Renaissance masters.

 A7 PIAZZA DI SANT'APOLLINARE 45 06-68-33-566

MUSEO PALATINO

The oldest inhabited site in the city, the building was home to patrician families during the Republican era. There's also an excavated settlement from the Iron Age, thought to date back to the 9th century B.C.

 D2 VIA DI SAN GREGORIO 30 06-69-90-110

MUSEO PIO-CLEMENTINO

The world's largest collection of classical statues spans 16 rooms at Museo Pio-Clementino. The Lacoön pieces are perhaps the most important group of antique sculptures due to their direct influence on Renaissance artists.

 B2 MUSEI VATICANI, VIALE VATICANO 06-69-88-38-60 OR 06-69-88-43-41

MUSEO PIO CRISTIANO

Obscure but fascinating early Christian antiquities – including sarcophagi of biblical stories – make up the exhibits at this part of the extensive Vatican Museum compound.

 B2 MUSEI VATICANI, VIALE VATICANO 06-69-88-38-60 OR 06-69-88-43-41

MUSEO STORICO-ARTISTICO E TESORO

Translated as a "historical-artistic" museum and treasury, this small space preserves Vatican artifacts gathered over the centuries, including a marble tabernacle by famed 15th-century Florentine sculptor Donatello.

 B2 MUSEI VATICANI, VIALE VATICANO 06-69-88-38-60 OR 06-69-88-43-41

MUSEO STORICO DELLA LIBERAZIONE DI ROMA

Located on the site where Nazis brought their prisoners for interrogation, this museum is a sobering and essential reminder of the atrocities of World War II.

 D6 VIA TASSO 145 06-70-03-866

MUSEO STORICO NAZIONALE DELL'ARTE SANITARIA

 The medieval medical artifacts at this compelling historical museum will make you appreciate modern medicine. Anatomical charts, which seem primitive today, are displayed along with early surgical tools.

 C4 LUNGOTEVERE IN SASSIA 3 06-68-93-051

PALAZZO CORSINI

 One of the best examples of baroque architecture in Rome, this palazzo houses a collection of art from the 16th and 17th centuries. The dramatic stone staircase alone is a reason to go.

 F5 VIA DELLA LUNGARA 10 06-68-80-23-23

SANTA MARIA DELLA CONCEZIONE

The crypt of this church is no ordinary burial place – the bones of some 4,000 Capuchin monks, separated into groups of like kind, have been arranged decoratively into patterns on the walls and ceilings.

 E6 VIA VENETO 27 06-48-71-185

SANTA MARIA SOPRA MINERVA

Built over the ruins of the Temple of Minerva, the ancient goddess of wisdom, this Gothic-style church contains many works of art from the Renaissance, including decorated tombs and Michelangelo's *Risen Christ*.

 D11 PIAZZA DELLA MINERVA 42 06-67-93-926

SOLIGO ART PROJECT

This modern and contemporary art gallery represents the work of such artists as Valeria Sanguini, Lidia Bachis, and Rita Tagliaferri.

 F1 VIA PANISPERNA 244 06-48-93-02-40

TERME DI DIOCLEZIANO

Diocletian's baths were the biggest in ancient Rome, able to accommodate 3,000 bathers at once. Only fragments remain, but it is possible to get a sense of the site's former grandeur by walking around the grounds.

 D2 VIALE E. DE NICOLA 79 06-47-82-61-52

▲

VILLA FARNESINA

Built in the early 16th century as a vacation home for powerful banker and Raphael patron Agostino Chigi, Villa Farnesina boasts Raphael-designed frescoes in its loggia.

 F6 VIA DELLA LUNGARA 230 06-68-80-17-67

PERFORMING ARTS

AUDITORIUM DI SANTA CECELIA

The home of the Accademia Nazionale di Santa Cecelia concert series since 1958 has poor acoustics but is perennially sold out nonetheless, thanks to devotees of the famed National Academy.

 C5 VIA DELLA CONCILIAZIONE 4
06-68-80-10-44

AUDITORIUM PARCO DELLA MUSICA

Italian architect Renzo Piano designed this striking musical complex located near Olympic Park in northern Rome. With a combined total of more than 7,000 seats, its three concert halls play host to operas, symphonies, and choirs.

OFF MAP VIA PIETRO DE COUBERTIN 15
06-80-241

AULA MAGNA DELL'UNIVERSITÀ DI ROMA LA SAPIENZA

Most concerts by the Instituzione Universitaria dei Concerti, founded after World War II, take place in this facist-designed space. Music programming varies widely from traditional to experimental.

 E6 PIAZZALE ALDO MORO 5
06-36-10-052

ESTATE ROMANA

The reason to be in the city in the summer (the name literally translates to Roman Summer), this extravaganza of theater performances, concerts, and films that runs June–September draws a world-class lineup, including performers such as Keith Jarrrett and George Benson. Signs all over town list individual events.

VARIOUS VENUES

PASQUINO

Long a favorite with American and British expats, this small, well-worn Trastevere cinema shows international films exclusively in their original languages – never dubbed – on its two screens.

 A3 PIAZZA SANT'EGIDIO 10
06-58-03-622

SALONE MARGHERITA

The performance menu here can range from political comedy to burlesque, and the atmosphere is lively, if not raucous.

 E4 VIA DUE MACELLI 75
06-67-91-439

SANTA MARIA DEGLI ANGELI

This is a popular venue for musical concerts. Since the Catholic Church doesn't allow paid programming at consecrated churches, all events are free to the public.

 D2 PIAZZA DELLA REPUBBLICA
06-48-80-812

▲

TEATRO ARGENTINA

Arguably the most popular in Rome, this theater is centrally located at the end of the tram line from Trastevere to *centro storico*. Productions range from Elizabethan plays in English to performances by Japanese dance companies.

 C5 LARGO ARGENTINA 52
06-68-80-46-01

TEATRO BELLI

 Small Teatro Belli devotes its stage to historically accurate and high-tech productions of contemporary Italian plays, many performed in their native dialects.

 B4 PIAZZA SANT'APOLLONIA 11
06-58-94-875

TEATRO COLOSSEO

A hip, two-stage theater frequented by Rome's twentysomethings, the Colosseo is a low-budget place with avant-garde productions by young Italian directors.

 D4 VIA CAPO D'AFRICA 5A
06-70-04-932

TEATRO DELLA COMETA

One of Rome's most unconventional theaters, the Cometa showcases original acting and writing talent from all over Italy. The space itself is tiny, making for intimate productions.

 C1 VIA DEL TEATRO MARCELLO 4 06-67-84-380

▲

TEATRO DELL'OPERA DI ROMA

An austere Mussolini façade belies the ornate 19th-century interior at Rome's main opera venue. This house stages world premieres – *Madama Butterfly* debuted here – and classic international works.

 E2 PIAZZA B. GIGLI 1 06-48-16-01

TEATRO DELL'OROLOGIO

Four small spaces spotlight experimental plays, mostly drama, in low-budget, but tightly organized, productions.

 D4 VIA DEI FILIPPINI 17A 06-68-30-87-35

TEATRO ELISEO – PICOLO ELISEO

This large, airy venue features the work of famous home-grown playwrights, such as Carlo Goldoni, as well as productions of Greek and British classics in Italian.

 B2 VIA NAZIONALE 183 06-48-82-114

TEATRO FLAIANO

 Best-known for staging Italian plays, this small, comfortable theater takes advantage of its good acoustics by also mounting excellent productions of famous operas with local performers.

 B7 VIA SANTO STEFANO DEL CACCO 15 •06-67-96-496

TEATRO QUIRINO

Large enough for grand-scale productions, this state-owned theater mounts mostly tried-and-true international dramas performed by Italian actors. The once famously bad acoustics are now better than average.

 A1 VIA DELLE VERGINI 7 06-67-94-585

TEATRO ROMANO DI OSTIA ANTICA

This beautifully preserved ancient amphitheater just a short train ride from the city hosts performances of traditional Greek and Roman classic plays. The seats are made of stone, so bring a cushion.

OFF MAP VIALE DEI ROMAGNOLI 717 06-56-35-80-99

TEATRO SISTINA

Often unintentionally camp, Teatro Sistina is home to the best of the city's musicals and always fun, even when productions are artistically lightweight. Local musicians occasionally perform acoustic shows, too.

 E5 VIA SISTINA 129 06-42-00-711

TEATRO XX SECOLO

 Despite its now-dated name, the 20th Century Theater presents fresh work by contemporary playwrights. Its location is dramatic in itself – it sits by one of Gianicolo's most picturesque fountains.

 B2 VIA GARIBALDI 30 06 58-81-637

TEATRO VITTORIA

This venue has two specialties: theater for children and international productions, many in English, for adults. The cavelike space makes for great sound.

 E5 PIAZZA SANTA MARIA LIBERATRICE 8 •06-57-40-170

NIGHTLIFE

AKAB

This large, bilevel club puts on popular weekend R&B shows featuring international talent. Weeknights are quieter, with performances by local bands of all kinds. Be prepared to wait in line, especially on Saturday nights.

OVERVIEW MAP F3 VIA DI MONTE TESTACCIO 69 • 06-57-57-494

ALEXANDERPLATZ

One of the city's most respected jazz clubs, Alexanderplatz spotlights famous musicians from Europe and the United States. Reservations are required, and dining at the club beforehand will secure better seats.

OVERVIEW MAP B1 VIA OSTIA 9 06-39-74-21-71

ALIEN

This loud club draws a twentysomething crowd with house and revival music. Saturdays bring a predominantly gay and lesbian clientele and feature gender-segregated musical events.

 A3 VIA VELLETRI 13 06-84-12-212

ALPHEUS

World music headlines Alpheus's auditory menu. Named Mississippi, Momotombo, Kiang, and Red River, the four stages inside this former Testaccio cheese factory host live performances and disco weekends.

OVERVIEW MAP F3 VIA DEL COMMERCIO 36 06-57-47-826

▲

ANIMA

Bartenders serve up creative cocktails and strong drinks in this deafening, crowded – you'll practically be sitting on someone's lap – funky bar where everyone qualifies as eye candy.

 D7 VIA DI SANTA MARIA DEL-L'ANIMA 8 • 06-68-64-661

BAR DEL FICO

Sit at a table surrounding the central fig tree, and enjoy a drink in one of the loveliest outdoor settings in Rome. Their art and photo exhibits add to the aesthetic atmosphere.

 C6 PIAZZA DEL FICO 27 06-68-65-205

BAR DELLA PACE

Local musicians, excellent wines by the glass, and a pick-up vibe are the fare at this after-hours bar. The outdoor tables are close together, but the night sky softens the acoustics.

 B6 VIA DELLA PACE 4 06-68-61-216

BIG MAMA

A highly regarded blues and jazz club, this tiny Trastevere haunt also offers R&B and African music. If you plan to see more than one show, opt for the well-priced annual membership.

 C4 VICOLO DI SAN FRANCESCO A. RIPA 18 • 06-58-12-551

BLUE CHEESE FACTORY

Located in a former bocce arena, Blue Cheese Factory is arguably the most popular club on Monte Testaccio. The well-attended Club Bluecheese takes over two rooms on Saturday nights, and British bands play at least once a month.

OVERVIEW MAP F3 VIA CAIO CESTO 513 06-57-25-00-32

BUSH

Rome's hottest techno club really comes alive after midnight, when well-heeled, *mojito*-sipping thirty-somethings drop in for the latest in international electronica.

 F5 VIA GALVANI 46 06-57-28-86-91

CAFFÈ LATINO

The hub of Rome's Latin music scene, Caffè Latino features three distinct spaces for its stylish, late-

night crowd – an upscale bar, a stage for live concerts, and a quieter room that screens music videos.
OVERVIEW MAP F3 VIA DI MONTE TESTACCIO 96 • 06-57-28-85-56

CARUSO
This dance club stages salsa and Latin American acts, while Saturday nights are devoted to disco. Filled with hip young things enjoying the inexpensive drinks, Caruso is never quiet enough for conversation.
OVERVIEW MAP F3 VIA DI MONTE TESTACCIO 36 • 06-57-45-019

DOME ROCK CAFÉ
Featuring live music every weekend, Dome Rock caters to British expats and English-speaking visitors. There's a good selection of beers on tap and knowledgeable servers to help you choose one.
 E6 VIA DOMENICO FONTANA 18 06-70-45-24-36

THE DRUNKEN SHIP
 Come here for an inexpensive beer around Campo dei Fiori and try to nab an outdoor table. You'll find tourists mixed in with the young crowd and good deejays spinning alternative tunes.
 C3 CAMPO DEI FIORI 20 06-68-30-05-35

FIDDLER'S ELBOW
The oldest Irish pub in the city has a loyal following of local expats and annual visitors. Jovial bartenders dispense great inexpensive beers, and most can speak a few sentences in many languages.
 F2 VIA DELL'OLMATA 43 06-48-72-110

FONCLEA
 A rare nonsmoking bar in this smokers' city, Fonclea provides an authentic pub atmosphere nonetheless. Couples and fevered intellectuals fill the cavelike cellar and nightly live music offerings tend toward jazz, R&B, and Latin.
 B4 VIA CRESCENZIO 82A 06-68-96-302

THE GALLERY
This fairly mainstream club features a psychedelic orange-and-blue décor and a rotating lineup of music genres (hip-hop Tuesdays, salsa- and merengue-flavored weekends). The touristy clientele gives off an ultra-friendly vibe.
 A10 VIA DELLA MADDALENA 12 06-68-72-316

GILDA
 This chic piano bar is a quiet after-hours alternative to Rome's club scene. Pricey cocktails, wine by the glass, and separate disco-and-dancing space draw a middle-aged clientele.
 E4 VIA MARIO DEI FIORI 97 06-67-84-838

HANGAR
An American-owned gay bar near the Colosseum, Hangar bustles on weekends, while a quiet date ambience prevails on weeknights. Men of all ages are the majority here, but women are also welcome.
 C4 VIA IN SELCI 69 06-48-81-397

HARRY'S BAR
Named after the Venetian original, this elegant, expensive bar and restaurant hosts the Via Veneto set. Sip a Bellini while listening to the lovely piano music.
 C6 VIA VENETO 150 06-47-42-103

HOTEL DE RUSSIE
This hotel bar is a great stop for a pre-dinner glass of champagne or a nightcap, even if you're not a guest. The air is sometimes smoky, but the lounge seating is nap-inducingly comfortable.
B2 VIA DEL BABUINO 9 06-21-88-81

HOTEL EDEN

Adjacent to the excellent La Terrazza restaurant, this bar has the same panoramic view of Rome for only the price of a cocktail. Patrons are treated to nightly piano music and fine service as well.

 D5 VIA LUDOVISI 49
06-47-81-21

JACKIE O.

As elegant as the former first lady herself, this space is often rented out for private functions. When it's open, you'll find a disco and piano bar filled with a 30s crowd dressed to impress. Reservations recommended on weekends.

 C1 VIA BONCOMPAGNI 11
06-42-88-54-57

JAZZ CAFÉ

With live jazz every night except Monday, this street-level café is a popular choice among the young and affluent for after-dinner drinks, while the mahogany bar downstairs is quiet enough to have a conversation.

 A7 VIA ZANARDELLI 12
06-68-61-990

JONATHAN'S ANGELS

 Dressed up in loud colors, theme decorations, and contemporary paintings, Jonathan's Angels boasts décor as vivid as its animated atmosphere. Drop a coin in the bathroom fountain for good luck.

 C6 VIA DELLA FOSSA 16
06-68-93-426

L'ALIBI

Among Rome's best gay bars, L'Alibi opens its wonderful roof garden in the summer and plays disco and alternative music on its high-tech sound system year-round. The expensive cover includes your first drink.

OVERVIEW MAP F3 VIA DI MONTE TES-TACCIO 44 • 06-57-43-448

IL LOCALE

Performing at Il Locale is what many local bands would consider their big break. Featuring only original music, this small club is packed to capacity, and sometimes beyond, every night.

 C5 VICOLO DEL FICO 3
06-68-79-075

NOTORIOUS

With its central location and good deejays, minuscule Notorious – possibly the smallest disco in Rome – is packed every night with twenty- and thirtysomething locals, as well as some in-the-know tourists.

 E6 VIA SAN NICOLA DA
TOLENTINO 22 • 06-42-01-05-72

RADIO LONDRA

More subdued than its clubby neighbors, this ultrcasual space has a café atmosphere. Deejays or occasional live acts generate blues, rock, and dance tunes for Radio Londra's friendly patrons.

OVERVIEW MAP F3 VIA DI MONTE TES-TACCIO 65B • 06-57-50-044

RIPARTÉ

Spare décor, wood floors, contemporary art, and low lights set the urban tone of this bar inside Rome's trendiest hotel. After 10 P.M. beautiful locals fill the space until the crowd spills out onto the street.

 D3 VIA DEGLI ORTI DI TRASTE-VERE 1 • 06-58-611

TRINITY COLLEGE

Many nights at the Italian-owned and -operated Trinity College end with patrons singing Irish ballads. The bartenders, who will remember your name if you visit more than once, add to the pub-like atmosphere.

 A1 VIA DEL COLLEGIO ROMANO 6
06-67-86-472

I VITELLONI

 A no-frills venue for music of all kinds, this club draws serious music fans with new local acts and out-of-town bands.

 D4 VIA SAN GIOVANNI IN
LATERANO 142 • 34-74-47-81-67

OUTDOORS

ARA PACIS

The altar of peace − a cubelike structure decorated with intricate friezes − was built in 19 B.C. to celebrate Augustus's victories in Gaul and Spain. This monument is visible during construction of a Richard Meier-designed museum around it.

 D2 VIA RIPETTA
06-36-00-34-71

ARCO DI CONSTANTINO

Built in A.D. 315, this grand arch celebrates Constantine's victory over his rival Maxentius at the Milvian Bridge. An early product of recycling, it was made from marble taken from older monuments that were no longer popular.

 D3 PIAZZA DEL COLOSSEO

ARCO DI GIANO

A tribute to Janus, the Roman god of new beginnings, this arch, with its solid, blocklike structure, is one of the least mentioned, but most imposing, monuments near Piazza Venezia.

 D1 PIAZZA DI SANT'ANASTASIA

CAMPO DEI FIORI

See SIGHTS, p. 3.

 C3 PIAZZA CAMPO DEI FIORI

CHIESA DEL GESÙ

 Il Gesù's austere façade − admired as a precursor to later baroque structures − belies its sumptuous interior. Frescoes by Il Baciccia and the ornate Chapel of St. Ignatius are two highlights of this main church of the Jesuits.

 C7 PIAZZA DEL GESÙ
06-69-70-01

CIRCO MASSIMO

 Once a massive ancient Roman stadium used for chariot races and executing criminals, this 650-yard athletic field is now a jogging track. Few ruins remain, so its history is invisible to the average passerby.

 E2 VIALE AVENTINO BTWN. VIA DEL CIRCO MASSIMO AND VIA DEL CERCHI

COLOSSEO

See SIGHTS, p. 7.

 D3 PIAZZA DEL COLOSSEO
06-39-96-77-00 OR 06-70-05-469

DOMUS AUREA

 This site contains the few remaining pieces of Nero's Golden House; the ruins are vivid enough to conjure images of its former glory, when its façade was made of gold and the baths were filled with seawater.

 C4 VIA DELLA DOMUS AUREA
06-39-96-77-00

FONTANA DELL'ACQUA FELICE

This fountain features a trio of arches that shelter sculptures of water-themed biblical stories. The middle statue of Moses, by Prospero Bresciano, suffers from an unfavorable comparison to Michelangelo's work in San Pietro in Vincoli.

 D1 PIAZZA SAN BERNARDO

FONTANA DELLE TARTARUGHE

The playful image of boys holding water-spewing dolphins sets the scene of this beloved fountain. Bernini is thought to have added the namesake turtles in the 17th century.

 D6 PIAZZA MATTEI

FONTANA DI TREVI

See SIGHTS, p. 8.

 F4 PIAZZA DI TREVI

FORO DI TRAIANO
See SIGHTS, p. 10.

 B2 VIA IV NOVEMBRE 94
06-67-90-048

FORO ROMANO
See SIGHTS, p. 11.

 C2 VIA DEI FORI IMPERIALI
06-69-90-110

FORUM BOARIUM
An open space near the Tiber, the Forum Boarium was once home to Rome's large meat and fish market. The two small temples standing in this area are the best-preserved temples from the 2nd and 3rd centuries B.C.

 D1 PIAZZA DELLA BOCCA DELLA VERITÀ

IL GALAPPATOIO

 Rent a horse for a gallop around this circular track in Villa Borghese park – it's the only riding facility inside Rome's city limits.

 B5 VIA DEL GALAPPATOIO 25
06-32-00-487

▲

GIANICOLO
The Gianicolo (Janiculum Hill) affords Romans the best view of their fair city. On a clear day you can see for miles; at night, the area becomes lovers' lane.

 B1 ENTER AT VIA GARIBALDI AND VIA DI GIANICOLO

GIARDINI VATICANI
The meticulously manicured Vatican Gardens contain statues, lakes, fountains, and of course, numerous flowers. A complete tour of the 40-acre grounds can take several hours.

 C1 CENTRO SERVIZI, PIAZZA DI SAN PIETRO 06-69-88-44-66

ISOLA TIBERINA
Dedicated to Aesculapius, the god of medicine, in 293 B.C., the sole island in the Tiber is a wonderful place for a picnic on the riverbank.

 A5 ACCESS VIA PONTE CESTIO

MAUSOLEO DI AUGUSTO
Though crumbling and trash-spotted, this circular monument is nonetheless the tomb of Augustus and his family. Tours during the week are by appointment only.

 D2 PIAZZA AUGUSTO IMPERATORE
06-67-10-38-19

MONTE PALATINO
See SIGHTS, p. 11.

 D2 VIA DI SAN GREGORIO 20
06-69-90-110

LA MOSCHEA DI ROMA
This 20th-century architectural masterpiece by Paolo Portoghesi is Rome's only mosque. Non-Muslims can visit on Wednesdays and Saturdays 9-11:30 A.M.

OFF MAP VIALE DELLA MOSCHEA 85
06-80-82-167

ORTO BOTANICO

 This lush expanse behind Palazzo Corsini includes thousands of plant species and a fascinating garden of scents and tactile sensations for the blind.

 A2 LARGO CRISTINA DI SVEZIA 24
06-68-64-193

PALAZZO DEL QUIRINALE
Originally a papal summer escape in the late 16th century, this grand residence, with its majestic door by Bernini and panoramic city views, has been beautifully preserved and is open to the public on Sunday mornings.

 A2 PIAZZA DEL QUIRINALE
06-46-991

PIAZZA DEI CAVALIERI DI MALTA
This lovely, walled piazza offers a delightful optical illusion. Peer through the tiny keyhole and see an up-close view of St. Peter's Basilica in miniature – an effect created by the arrangement of trees along the

walkway leading to the headquarters of the Knights of Malta.

 D6 PIAZZA DEI CAVALIERI DI MALTA

PIAZZA DEL CAMPIDOGLIO
See SIGHTS, p. 15.

 C1 INTERSECTION OF VIA DEL TEATRO DI MARCELLO, VIA DELLE TRE PILE, VIA DEL CAMPIDOGLIO, AND VIA SAN PIETRO IN CARLERE
06-67-10-20-71

PIAZZA DELLA BOCCA DELLA VERITÀ
In the courtyard of the Church of Santa Maria in Cosmedin, the "Mouth of Truth" is said to bite the hand of anyone who dares to lie in its presence. In truth, it is an ornate drain cover.

 D1 VIA L. PETROSELLI

▲

PIAZZA DELLA REPUBBLICA
At the center of this prominent piazza is the Fontana delle Naiadi, adorned with a bronze sculpture of women – controversial when first presented in 1901 due to their nudity – wrestling with sea creatures.

 D2 PIAZZA DELLA REPUBBLICA

▲

PIAZZA DEL POPOLO
Giuseppe Valadier designed this enormous, busy piazza between 1818 and 1822. The northern boundary of the city center, it features a stately obelisk and two churches, Santa

Maria dei Miracoli and Santa Maria del Popolo.

 B2 PIAZZA DEL POPOLO

PIAZZA DI SPAGNA
See SIGHTS, p. 16.

 D4 INTERSECTION OF VIA DEL BABUINO, VIA CONDOTTI, AND PIAZZA TRINITÀ DEI MONTI

PIAZZA NAVONA
See SIGHTS, p. 18.

 C7 INTERSECTION OF VIA AGO-NALE, CORSIA AGONALE, VIA DELLA CUCCAGNA, AND VIA DI SANT'AGNESE

PONTE SANT'ANGELO
Arguably the city's most beautiful bridge, the Sant'Angelo is lined with good copies of Bernini's angels – the originals have been moved to the Church of Sant'Andrea delle Fratte for more certain preservation.

 C5 LUNGOTEVERE CASTELLO

QUATTRO FONTANE
 Representing the Tiber, Arno, Juno, and Diana, four baroque fountains – one on each corner – mark this intersection. Sadly, air pollution has damaged the landmarks.

 E1 VIA DELLE QUATTRO FONTANE AT VIA DEL QUIRINALE

ROMARENT
Located in the center of the Campo dei Fiori neighborhood, this bike and Vespa outfitter offers reasonably priced guided tours of the city, such as an excursion through the ancient ruins outside the city walls.

 B3 VICOLO DEI BOVARI 7A
06-68-96-555

SAN CRISOGONO
The portico of this church is decorated with eagles and dragons, symbols of the Borghese family. Parts of San Crisogono date back to the 5th century; today it's a community center of sorts in Trastevere.

 B4 PIAZZA SONNINO 44
06-58-18-225

SANTA MARIA IN COSMEDIN
Built in the 6th century for Rome's growing Greek population, this

church shares its piazza with the Bocca della Verità and is recognized in its own right by its elegant landmark belfry.

 D1 PIAZZA BOCCA DELLA VERITÀ 06-67-81-419

▲

SANTA MARIA MAGGIORE
One of four great pilgrimage churches in the city, St. Mary Major, built in A.D. 440, is one of the oldest as well. Its design combines Romanesque, baroque, and other styles, and the interior mosaics are breathtaking.

 F2 PIAZZA SANTA MARIA MAGGIORE 06-48-81-094

SANT'ANDREA AL QUIRINALE
Completed in 1670, this unusual church of pink marble is a striking example of Bernini's architecture. Step inside to admire the clever oval floor plan.

 F6 VIA DEL QUIRINALE 29 06-48-90-31-87

SANTI COSMA E DAMIANO
Originally a Roman structure belonging to Vespasian's forum of peace, this 6th-century church features frescoes by Francesco Allegrini.

 C3 VIA DEI FORI IMPERIALI 1 06-69-20-441

SCALA SANTA
Brought to Rome by Constantine's mother, St. Helena, from Pilate's palace in Jerusalem, these holy steps are to be ascended while kneeling and lead to a chapel containing sacred relics.

 E6 PIAZZA DI SAN GIOVANNI IN LATERANO 14 • 06-77-26-641

SCOOTERS FOR RENT
 With choices ranging from motorcycle-like to puttering, this shop near Villa Borghese will set you up with a Vespa for tooling around the city on two motorized wheels.

 E5 VIA DELLA PURIFICAZIONE 84 06-48-85-485

TEATRO DI MARCELLO
Begun by Julius Caesar and completed by Augustus in A.D. 13, this former theater is among the more interesting ruins in Rome because you can explore it with little restriction.

 F7 VIA DEL TEATRO DI MARCELLO

TERME DI CARACALLA
See SIGHTS, p. 21.
OVERVIEW MAP E4 VIA DELLE TERME DI CARACALLA 52 • 06-57-58-626

TORRE ARGENTINA CAT SANCTUARY
The sacred ruins in the area where Caesar was killed has been home to hundreds of abandoned cats since 1994, when a group of feline-friendly volunteers started this sanctuary.

 C5 TORRE ARGENTINA 06-68-72-133

VILLA ADA
A popular park among local runners, the Villa Ada is just north of the city center and has refreshingly peaceful ponds and lakes.
OVERVIEW MAP A5 VIA SALARIA

VILLA BORGHESE
See SIGHTS, p. 22.
 C6 MAIN ENTRANCE AT PIAZZALE BRASILE

VILLA CELIMONTANA
One of the loveliest public parks in Rome, this villa on Celian Hill was once owned by the Mattei family, who contributed much of the art on display in Palazzo Altemps. There's a lush garden and swings for the kids.

 E4 PIAZZA NAVICELLA

VILLA DORIA PAMPHILJ
The major park on the south side of Rome, this open space has numerous jogging trails, as well as picnic spots and play areas for kids.
OVERVIEW MAP D1 VIA DI SAN PANCRAZIO

Ⓗ HOTELS

CHIC HOTELS

RIPA HOTEL
This least Roman of Roman hotels, with its seedy side-street location and postindustrial façade, gives a dubious first impression. Once inside, however, the cool, minimalist décor is a balm in this city steeped in history. Rooms are spare, with recessed lighting and ergonomic chairs – there's not an antique in sight. The staff is young, pretty, and eminently professional, and the on-site restaurant is one of the hottest in town. $$

 D3 VIA DEGLI ORTI DI TRASTEVERE 1
06-58-611

BAILEY'S
Modern elegance is the theme here, and marble is the medium. The full suite of amenities includes fast Internet connections, a here-to-please staff, and touches like fresh flowers. $$

 C2 VIA FLAVIA 39
06-42-02-04-86

CASA HOWARD
Popular with people in the film industry, this is a playground for the jet set. All the furnishings are one-of-a-kind designs, and the Chinese Room, with its Turkish bath, is exquisite. $

 E5 VIA CAPO LE CASE 18
06-69-92-45-55

DEI BORGOGNONI
Amazingly quiet for its proximity to Rome's shopping corridor, this small hotel is within walking distance of most major sights in the city. Rooms are both comfortable and elegant. $$

 F4 VIA DEL BUFALO 126
06-69-94-15-05

HOTEL DE RUSSIE
Luxe Hotel de Russie boasts Rome's best spa and a decidedly 21st-century, as opposed to antique, appeal. The beautiful lobby bar is an evening destination for locals and travelers alike. $$$

 B2 VIA DEL BABUINO 9
06-32-88-81

HOTEL TIZIANO
The best choice for upscale lodging near Campo dei Fiori, the Tiziano is both luxurious (Egyptian cotton linens) and practical (English-speaking staff). $$

 B5 CORSO VITTORIO EMANUELE II 110 • 06-68-65-019

LOCARNO
The Locarno has two distinct wings: an older, more traditional section and a contemporary all-suites addition. Both are inviting and accompanied by impeccable service. $$

C2 VIA DELLA PENNA 22
06-36-10-841

LORD BYRON
One of the city's few art deco hotels, this town house borders the Villa Borghese, and the discreet service is a treat for the demanding, stylish clientele. $$$

OVERVIEW MAP A3 VIA G. DE NOTARIS 5
06-32-20-404

PARCO DEI PRINCIPI
Parco dei Principi's location away from the center of town provides for spacious rooms and a beautiful swimming pool, a rarity in this cramped city. Deluxe rooms come with views of Villa Borghese and St. Peter's. $$$

OVERVIEW MAP A4 VIA G. FRESCOBALDI 5
06-85-44-21

RESIDENZA CELLINI
Once the home of a countess, Residenza Cellini offers six exceptionally large, light-filled rooms. Beds come with orthopedic mattresses, and many bathrooms have hot tubs. $$

 E1 VIA MODENA 5
06-47-82-52-04

GRAND HOTELS

CAVALIERI HILTON

Perched on one of Rome's seven hills, the world's most Italianate Hilton delivers luxury and privacy with old-world formality (think personal concierge), without neglecting modern comforts like 24-hour room service. Heinz Beck's restaurant, La Pergola, is reason alone to stay here. If the glorious views from every balcony weren't tempting you to go into the city, which is three miles away, there'd be no reason to leave the premises. $$$

OFF MAP VIA CADLOLO 101
06-35-091

ATLANTE STAR

The grandest hotel near St. Peter's, the Atlante Star draws even non-guests to its 5,000-square-foot roof garden with a panoramic view of the city. The antique-filled rooms have marble bathrooms, each with a hot tub. $$

 B4 VIA VITELLESCHI 34
06-68-73-233

DE LA VILLE INTER-CONTINENTAL

This hotel claims to have Rome's highest percentage of repeat guests, some going back several generations. Regulars receive first dibs on booking specific rooms. The lobby is extravagant, but the rooms are austere. $$$

 E5 VIA SISTINA 67
06-67-331

EMPIRE PALACE HOTEL

The spacious rooms here feature original contemporary paintings and are furnished with tasteful antiques. The hotel's bar draws a local crowd for drinks every night. $$

 C2 VIA AURELIANA 39
06-42-12-81

EXCELSIOR

One of the most lavish hotels in Rome, the Excelsior could be in Hollywood. It attracts Italy's most extroverted elite with its crystal chandeliers, gargantuan flower arrangements, and deferential service. $$$

 D6 VIA VENETO 125
06-47-081

HOTEL EDEN

The Eden, Fellini's favorite hotel in Rome, is the epitome of casual elegance with its understated, even conservative, rooms. La Terrazza, the hotel's main restaurant, is a destination in itself. $$$

 D5 VIA LUDOVISI 49
06-47-81-21

MAJESTIC

A throwback to the 19th century, complete with original antiques, the Majestic takes service seriously, while avoiding pretension. Stop in at the bar for a surprising soundtrack of '70s pop music. $$$

 D6 VIA VENETO 50
06-42-14-41

PLAZA

Built in 1860, the Plaza, with its fin de siècle ambience, has changed little since. Rooms are furnished with original antique pieces, but guests can expect 21st-century amenities. $$$

 E3 VIA DEL CORSO 126
06-69-92-11-11

REGINA BAGLIONI

The sumptuous lobby here flaunts oriental rugs, silk wall coverings, and original antiques; the exceptionally large rooms are just as ornate. $$$

 D6 VIA VENETO 72
06-42-11-11

ST. REGIS GRAND

Every room at the St. Regis has a hand-painted fresco above the bed. The lobby contains chandeliers made of Murano glass, and the service lives up to the elegance. $$$

 D1 VIA VITTORIO EMANUELE
ORLANDO 3 • 06-47-091

QUAINT HOTELS

GREGORIANA HOTEL
Located in the most coveted neighborhood in Rome, the Gregoriana is also the Tridente's best value. The small rooms are soundproof and spare, but avoid being austere with interior touches like lush red fabrics. While there's no on-site restaurant, an attentive staff delivers breakfast every morning. $

 D4 VIA GREGORIANA 18
06-67-97-988

BERNINI BRISTOL
A Roman favorite since 1870, the Bristol is synonymous with old-world gentility and hospitality. The rooms are opulent without being gaudy, and the service is flawless. $$

 E6 VIA BARBERINI 23
06-48-83-051

CESARI
This small, quiet hotel is invested in preserving its history, which dates back to the mid-1800s when Stendhal was a frequent guest. Only the interior has ever been renovated and now sports muted hues and marble bathrooms. $$

 B12 VIA DI PIETRA 89A
06-67-49-701

DOMUS AVENTINA
A very Roman hotel, even down to the classical artifacts in the lobby, with well-appointed rooms, this small, gracious establishment is a good base for exploring the city's major archaeological sites. $

 F1 PIAZZA DI SANTA PRISCA 11B
06-57-46-135

HOTEL PORTOGHESI
This tiny hotel has a roof garden with one of the biggest views of Rome. Rooms are small but generously furnished with copies of period antiques, and the service is friendly and discreet. $

 F1 VIA DEI PORTOGHESI 1
06-68-64-231

SANTA CHIARA
The same family has lovingly owned and operated this bastion of hospitality for more than 150 years. Small rooms offer marble desks and baths, and several overlook a lovely piazza. $

 D10 VIA SANTA CHIARA 21
06-68-72-979

SCALINATA DI SPAGNA
One of the best values near pricey Piazza di Spagna, this hotel is easy to miss, even though it's right at the top of the steps. With a mere 16 rooms, it's perennially booked months in advance. $$

 D4 PIAZZA DELLA TRINITÀ DEI MONTI 17 • 06-67-93-006

SOLE AL PANTHEON
This is the only hotel in Rome that can claim the Pantheon as its next-door neighbor. Rooms are small, but high ceilings and tile floors add to the illusion of space. $$

 C10 PIAZZA DELLA ROTONDA 63
06-67-80-441

TEATRO DI POMPEO
Ancient architecture and contemporary hospitality come together at Teatro di Pompeo, which is built on the site of Julius Caesar's assassination. Guest rooms have original beams from the 15th century. $

 C3 LARGO DEL PALLARO 8
06-80-55-31

VILLA SAN PIO
The décor is ornate Venetian, in contrast to the hotel's location close to Rome's best archaeological sites. Guests can enjoy manicured gardens and get lost amidst grape arbors hidden on the grounds. $

 E6 VIA SANTA MELANIA 19
06-57-83-214

ROMANTIC HOTELS

HOTEL RAPHAËL

From the original Picasso ceramics in the lobby to the guest rooms individually designed by Florentine masters, this centrally located hideaway beckons those who seek true privacy – or even secrecy – behind its opaque curtains and mysterious doors. One of Rome's top hotels, the Raphaël lulls guests with perfect service and attention to detail. The classic surroundings also accommodate modern luxuries, like a large gym. **$$$**

 B7 LARGO FEBO 2
06-68-28-31

ALBERGO DEL SOLE AL BISCIONE

Built near the ruins of the Teatro di Pompeo, this updated pension offers unparalleled views of Campo dei Fiori. With 58 rooms, the hotel feels like a cozy inn. **$**

 B3 VIA DEL BISCIONE 76
06-68-80-68-73

BRAMANTE

The perfect outpost for a Vatican-centered visit, the Bramante offers privacy and personalized service. The high-ceilinged rooms are elegantly spare. **$**

 C4 VICOLO DELLE PALLINE 24
06-68-80-64-26

DUCA D'ALBA

The neoclassical décor here is stylishly elegant. The soundproof rooms all have custom-made furnishings, and the bathrooms are outfitted in Carrara marble. **$**

 C3 VIA LEONINA 14
06-48-44-71

HASSLER VILLA MEDICI

The most famous hotel at the top of the Spanish Steps, the Hassler has stunning views of the Eternal City. It has the air of nonchalant extravagance, from the classically decorated guest rooms to the discreet service. **$$$**

 D4 PIAZZA DELLA TRINITÀ DEI MONTI 6 • 06-69-93-40

HOTEL CELIO

More of an inn than a hotel, the Celio is a visually stunning space with original murals and custom furniture. Right behind the Colosseum, it's also a good base for touring the Roman Forum and Aventino. **$**

 D4 VIA DEI SANTI QUATTRO 35C
06-70-49-53-33

HOTEL D'INGHILTERRA

This property was once the home of Torlonia princes; today the small but luxurious rooms host weary shoppers. Complementing the stately décor is the hotel's highly regarded art collection. **$$**

 E3 VIA BOCCA DI LEONE 14
06-69-981

HOTEL VALADIER

Located between the Spanish Steps and Piazza del Popolo, this hotel offers opulent rooms, marble baths, and a rooftop terrace with panoramic views. The service is professional without being stuffy. **$$$**

 C2 VIA DELLA FONTANELLA 15
06-36-11-998

RESIDENZA ZANARDELLI

Silk wallpaper by Versace is an example of the elegant details inside this seven-room residence. The hosts creates an intimate atmosphere that is both familial and private. **$**

 A7 VIA ZANARDELLI 7
06-68-21-13-92

TREVI

Located on a side street near its namesake fountain, this little-known hotel is an oasis of tranquillity and privacy, despite being a mere 10-minute walk from the bustling Spanish Steps. **$**

 A1 VICOLO DEL BABUCCIO 21
06-67-89-563

CITY ESSENTIALS

LEONARDO DA VINCI AIRPORT (FIUMICINO)

Most international and domestic flights into Rome land at Fiumicino, approximately 20 miles south of the city. A special nonstop train, the most efficient way to get into the city, goes directly to Termini train station every 30 minutes. Tickets, available for purchase at automated machines in baggage claim and the main lobby, cost less than $10 and must be validated before boarding at the station platform. Buses also connect the airport to Tiburtina Station, from which you can take a subway or another bus into the center of town. Tickets must be purchased in advance, either from automated machines or *tabacchi,* and must be validated immediately after boarding. A taxi ride into the city center takes 30–45 minutes and will cost between $50 and $70.

PUBLIC TRANSPÓRTATION

Rome's public transportation system is inexpensive and very efficient. ATAC, Rome's transit system (06-46-951), operates buses and two metro (subway) lines, and tickets are the same for each. Bus tickets must be validated on board, while metro tickets are validated at turnstiles in the station. Bus tickets are good for unlimited transfers during a 75-minute period, and metro tickets are good for one transfer. Weeklong passes are available for less than $15.

The subway stops running at 11:30 P.M. on weekdays and 12:30 A.M. on weekends. Most buses run until midnight. Night buses bear a night owl logo on them. You can pick up bus and subway maps at newsstands.

TAXIS

All licensed taxis have meters (refuse a ride if there isn't one), and rates start at $2.40, increasing incrementally according to time and distance. There's an extra charge of €1 (about $1) for each piece of luggage placed in the trunk. Tipping usually constitutes simply rounding up to the next euro. There are taxi stands in major tourist areas, and you can call for one as well. Flagging one down is possible but is not the most effective way of getting a ride.

DRIVING AND RENTING A CAR

U.S. driver's licenses are valid in Italy. Rental car prices vary widely, ranging $18-40 per day, not including hefty taxes that run upwards of 20 percent. Driving in Rome is a difficult proposition, as lanes tend not to be honored, and Vespas, which seem to be everywhere, make their own rules. Parking, too, is difficult. Some neighborhoods have metered parking, while others are restricted from car traffic altogether. Public garages are not only expensive, but there are very few of them in the city center.

The major international rental companies are all represented in Rome, as are many locally owned companies. Many are closed on Sundays, except at the airport and Termini Station, so make sure your branch is open when you plan to pick up and return your vehicle.

AVIS 06-65-95-41-46 (AIRPORT), 19-91-00-133 (INFORMATION)

HERTZ 06-54-29-41 (AIRPORT), 19-91-12-211 (INFORMATION)

CURRENCY EXCHANGE

Most banks in Rome are open Mon.-Fri. 9 A.M.-5 P.M., though some still close for lunch for about an hour starting at 1:30 P.M. Commissions on currency exchange vary; some charge a percentage, while others charge a flat fee. All banks other than commercial ones will exchange foreign currency, and most will cash traveler's checks and give cash advances to Visa cardholders.

Thomas Cook and American Express are the two most widely represented exchange bureaus in Rome. The former has a branch at the airport, and both have branches in several central locations in the city.

AMERICAN EXPRESS

 D4 PIAZZA DI SPAGNA 38
06-67-641

THOMAS COOK

 E6 PIAZZA BARBERINI 21
06-42-02-01-50

EMBASSIES

BRITISH EMBASSY

 B3 VIA XX SETTEMBRE 80A
06-48-25-441

CANADIAN EMBASSY

 A6 VIA G.B. DE ROSSI 27
06-44-59-81

U.S. EMBASSY

 D6 VIA VENETO 119A
06-46-741

WEATHER

Rome is hot and humid in summer, when temperatures can reach well into the 90s. Spring and fall are mild, and most of the city's rainfall occurs in March, April, and September. Winters are also mild, with average temperatures staying in the 50s, though many public spaces aren't heated.

HOURS

Rome is not a particularly late-night city, especially where dining is concerned. Restaurants usually close around 1 A.M. and usually don't have reservations after 11 P.M. Neighborhoods with the greatest concentration of after-hours bars and cafés include Trastevere/Testaccio and Piazza Navona/Pantheon. In general, shops are open Mon.-Fri. 10 A.M.-1 P.M. and 4-7 P.M., though in tourist areas, many stay open all day. The majority of businesses of all kinds close for all or part of August.

DISABLED ACCESS

Rome is not a terribly accessible city as far as wheelchair ramps and sight access go. There are buses that accommodate wheelchair users, but it's important to call ATAC (06-70-30-52-48) ahead of time to check current availability and routes. There's also a helpful phone information line operated by TRAMBUS (06-71-28-96-76), with multilingual staffers who can answer questions about access.

SAFETY

Crime in Rome tends toward theft rather than more violent acts. Pickpockets are prevalent on crowded buses, and cars are often targets as well (always remove valuables). In general, use precaution when traveling in unfamiliar areas, especially at night. The area immediately around Termini Station is especially unsavory, with the highest crime rates in the city.

HEALTH AND EMERGENCY SERVICES

The general emergency number (free from any phone) is 113. If you need an ambulance, dial 118. The direct line for the fire department is 115. The police department also maintains a hot line in English at 112. Pharmacists are well-versed in prescription medications and can legally offer advice and help. They also routinely prescribe herbal and homeopathic remedies to treat minor ailments.

Don't leave home without ascertaining that your health insurance policy will cover you in Italy. Citizens of the E.U. are automatically covered, but U.S. residents must provide their own coverage.

PHARMACIES

Every pharmacy is required to post the nearest location that is open 24 hours or is at least on call for emergencies. This location rotates every week.

FARMACIA DELLA STAZIONE

 E3 PIAZZA DEI CINQUECENTO 51
06-48-80-019

FARMACIA INTERNAZIONALE BARBERINI

E6 PIAZZA BARBERINI 49
06-48-25-456

FARMACIA TRINITÀ DEI MONTI

D4 PIAZZA DI SPAGNA 30
06-67-90-626

PIRAM

E1 VIA NAZIONALE 228
06-48-80-754

MEDIA AND COMMUNICATIONS

All the phone numbers in this book are listed as they would be dialed within Rome. Rome telephone numbers do not have a set number of digits, but rather vary between five and eight. Most numbers begin with 06. Dial 12 for Italian directory assistance and 170 for an international operator.

You must buy a *scheda telefonica* if you need to use a pay phone. These are telephone cards with preset spending limits and are available at *tabacchi* in denominations as low as €2.50. International calls can be made with calling cards from pay phones without a *scheda,* provided you have a toll-free access number.

The Italian postal service has branches throughout Rome, identified with yellow signs. Normal hours are Mon.-Fri. 8:30 A.M.-2 P.M., and Sat. 8:30 A.M.-2 P.M. Main offices have pay phones, photocopy, and fax machines, and some even have ATM machines. Recently overhauled, the system is now much more efficient. Letter rates within Italy begin at €.41, while an international letter runs €.77.

Italy's main newspapers include *Corriere della Sera* and *La Repubblica.* The English-language *International Herald Tribune* (owned by *The New York Times*) is available at most newsstands in the city center and includes an insert, *Italy Weekly,* that features local news and events.

The phone number for general tourist information is 06-36-00-43-99. Information is available in English, and the hours of operation are daily 9 A.M.-7 P.M.

INTERNET

Most hotels offer Internet access in public areas for a nominal fee, though beware of hidden in-room charges. You can also stop in at one of these Internet cafés.

BIBLI

B4 VIA DEI FIENAROLI 28
06-58-84-097

EASY INTERNET

E6 VIA BARBERINI 2
06-42-90-33-88

THE NETGATE

F2 PIAZZA FIRENZE 25
06-68-79-098

SMOKING

Rome is a smoker's paradise. Nonsmoking sections in hotels, restaurants, and bars are virtually nonexistent. Sitting outside, rather than in closed quarters, is often the only viable answer for those who don't want to breathe secondhand smoke.

TIPPING

Most dining establishments include a 10-15 percent service charge in the bill, but it is customary to round up to the next euro, or even to add 5 percent more if service is superlative.

DRY CLEANERS

There's a dry cleaner on almost every corner in the city. If you can't find one, simply ask for a *tintoria* or *lavanderia.* Most hotels offer one-day service at slightly higher rates.

BOLLE BLU

C3 VIA PALESTRO 59
06-44-65-804

RITA TASELLI

C3 PIAZZA CAMPO DEI FIORI 38
06-68-79-096

WASH & DRY LAVARAPIDO

A3 VIA DELLA PELLICCIA 35
80-02-31-172

ITALIAN PHRASES

Known as the language of poetry and love, Italian is perhaps the most musical language in the world. Speaking it is both fun and theatrical (moving your hands becomes natural) and not very difficult, since in most cases, words are pronounced exactly as they are written. With so many tourists passing through their city, Romans are accustomed to hearing foreign tongues and accents and have an open and playful attitude about helping you speak their language. They are also eager to show off their ability to speak English. So relax and get used to saying the most common expression, *"va bene"* (it's going fine).

THE BASICS

ENGLISH	ITALIAN	PRONUNCIATION
Good day	Buon giorno	*bwon jor-no*
Good evening	Buona sera	*bwo-na say-ra*
Welcome	Benvenuto	*ben-ven-oo-to*
Excuse me	Mi scusi	*mee skoo-zee*
Pardon	Permesso	*per-mes-so*
Sir	Signore	*seen-yor-ay*
Madam	Signora	*seen-yor-ah*
Miss	Signorina	*seen-yor-ee-na*
Do you speak English?	Parla inglese?	*par-la een-glay ray*
I don't speak Italian	Non parlo italiano	*non par-lo ee-tal-ya-no*
How are you? (formal)	Come sta?	*ko-may sta*
Very well, thank you	Molto bene, grazie	*mole-tow be-nay grat-see-ay*
How's it going? (informal)	Come va?	*ko-may va*
It's going fine	Va bene	*va be-nay*
My name is...	Mi chiamo...	*mee kee-a-mo*
What's your name?	Come si chiama?	*ko-may see kee-a-ma*
Please	Per favore	*payr fa vor ray*
Thank you	Grazie	*grat-see-ay*
You're welcome	Prego	*pray-go*
I'm sorry	Mi dispiace	*mee dees-pee-ah-chay*
Goodbye	Arrivederci; ciao	*ar-ree-ve-der-chee; chow*
Yes	Sì	*see*
No	No	*no*

GETTING AROUND

How do I get to...?	Come posso andare a...	*ko-may pohs-so an-da-ray a...*
Where is...?	Dove	*do-vay*
the subway	la metro	*la met-ro*
the airport	l'aeroporto	*lay-ro-por-to*
the train station	la stazione di treno	*la stats-yo-nay dee tray-no*
the train	il treno	*eel tray-no*
the bus stop	la fermata dell'autobus	*la fair-ma-tah day-la-ow-to-boos*
the bus	l'autobus	*la ow-to-boos*
the exit	l'uscita	*le oo-shee-ta*
the street	la strada	*la stra-da*
the garden	il giardino	*eel jar-dee-no*
the tourist office	l'ufficio turistico	*loof-fee-cho too-rees-tee-ko*
a taxicab	un taxi	*oon tak-see*
a hotel	un albergo	*oon al-bair-go*
a toilet	la toilette	*la twa-let*
a pharmacy	una farmacia	*oo-na farm-a-chee-a*

| a bank | una banca | oo-na bang-ka |
| a telephone | un telefono | oon te-le-foh-no |

HEALTH AND EMERGENCY

Help!	Aiuto!	a-yoo-to
I am sick	Mi sento male	mee sen-to ma-lay
I am hurt	Mi sono fatto male	mee son-no fat-to ma-lay
I need...	Ho bisogno di...	o bee-zon-yo dee
the hospital	l'ospedale	los-pe-da-lay
a doctor	un medico	oon me-dee-ko
an ambulance	un'ambulanza	oon am-boo-lant-sa
the police	la polizia	la po-leet-see-a
medicine	medicina	me-dee-chee-nah

EATING

I would like...	Vorrei...	vor-ray
a table for two	un tavolo per due	oon ta-vo-lo payr doo-ay
the menu	il menù	eel me-noo
breakfast	la colazione	la ko-lats-yo-nay
lunch	pranzare	pron-tsar-ay
dinner	cenare	chey-nar-ay
the bill	il conto	eel kon-to
nonsmoking	non-fumatore	non foo-ma-to-ray
a drink	una bibite	oon-a bee-bee-tay
a glass of...	un bicchiere di..	oon beek-ye-ray dee
water	acqua	ak-wa
beer	birra	beer-ra
wine	vino	vee-no
I am...	Sono...	so-no
a vegetarian	vegetariano/a	ve-jay-ta-ree-a-no/a
diabetic	diabetico/a	dee-a-be-tee-ko/a
allergic	allergico/a	al-ler-jee-ko/a
kosher	kosher	ko-shur

SHOPPING

Do you have...?	Avete...?	a-vet-ay
Where can I buy...?	Dove posso comprare...?	do-vay pos-so kom-pra-ray
May I try this?	Potrei provarlo?	po-tray pro-var-lo
How much is this?	Quanto costa?	kwan-to kos-ta
cash	in contanti	een kon-tan-tee
credit card	la carta di credito	la kar-ta dee kre-dee-to
Too...	Troppo...	trohp-po
small	piccolo/a	peek-ko-lo/a
large	grande	gran-day
expensive	caro	ka-ro

TIME

What time is it?	Che ora sono?	kay or-a so-no
It is...	Sono...	so-no
eight o'clock	le otto	lay oht-toh
half past ten	le dieci e mezza	lay dee-ay-chee ay med-za
noon	mezzogiorno	med-zo jor-no
midnight	mezzanotte	med-za-noht-tay
during the day	durante il giorno	doo-ran-tay eel jor-no
in the morning	di mattina	dee mat-tee-na
in the afternoon	nel pomeriggio	nel po-may-reed-jo
in the evening	la sera	la say-ra
at night	a notte	a not-tay

DAYS OF THE WEEK

Monday	lunedì	*lee-ne-dee*
Tuesday	martedì	*mar-te-dee*
Wednesday	mercoledì	*mair-ko-le-dee*
Thursday	giovedì	*jo-ve-dee*
Friday	venerdì	*ven-air-dee*
Saturday	sabato	*sa-ba-toh*
Sunday	domenica	*do-me-nee-ka*
this week	questa settimana	*kwesta set-tee-ma-na*
this weekend	questo fine settimana	*kwest-o fi-nay set-tee-ma-na*
today	oggi	*oj-jee*
tomorrow	domani	*do-ma-nee*
yesterday	ieri	*yair-ee*

MONTHS

January	gennaio	*jen-na-yo*
February	febbraio	*feb-bra-yo*
March	marzo	*mart-zo*
April	aprile	*a-pree-lay*
May	maggio	*maj-jo*
June	giugno	*joon-yo*
July	luglio	*lool-yo*
August	agosto	*a-gos-toh*
September	settembre	*set-tem-bray*
October	ottobre	*ot-to-bray*
November	novembre	*no-vem-bray*
December	dicembre	*dee-chem-bray*
this month	questo mese	*kwest-o me-se*
this year	quest'anno	*kwest-an-no*
winter	inverno	*een-vair-no*
spring	primavera	*pree-ma-vair-a*
summer	estate	*es-ta-tay*
fall	autunno	*ow-toon-no*

NUMBERS

zero	zero	*dze-ro*
one	uno	*oo-no*
two	due	*doo-ay*
three	tre	*tray*
four	quattro	*kwat-troh*
five	cinque	*cheen-kway*
six	sei	*se-ee*
seven	sette	*set-tay*
eight	otto	*ot-toh*
nine	nove	*no-vay*
ten	dieci	*dyay-chee*
eleven	undici	*oon-dee-chee*
twelve	dodici	*do-dee-chee*
thirteen	tredici	*tray-dee-chee*
fourteen	quattordici	*kwat-tor-dee-chee*
fifteen	quindici	*kween-dee-chee*
sixteen	sedici	*se-dee-chee*
seventeen	diciasette	*dee-chias-set-tay*
eighteen	diciotto	*dee-chiot-to*
nineteen	dicianove	*dee-chian-no-vay*
twenty	venti	*ven-tee*
one hundred	cento	*chen-toh*
one thousand	mile	*meel-lay*

STREET INDEX

MOON METRO ROME
1ST EDITION

Published by
Avalon Travel Publishing
1400 65th Street, Suite 250
Emeryville, CA 94608, USA

Distributed by Publishers Group West

Text and maps © 2003 by Avalon Travel Publishing, Inc.
All rights reserved.

Grateful acknowledgment is made for reproduction permission:
ATAC S.p.A.: Rome Metro Map © 2003

ISBN: 1-56691-565-1
ISSN: 1543-1908

Editor: Grace Fujimoto
Series Manager: Grace Fujimoto
Design: Michele Harding
Production Coordinator: Jacob Goolkasian
Graphics Coordinator: Justin Marler
Cartographers: Suzanne Service, Mike Morgenfeld
Map Editor: Naomi Adler Dancis
Proofreader: Leslie Miller
Fact Checker: Kristine Crane
Indexer: Erika Howsare

Contributing Writer: Kim Westerman
Phrasebook: Kristine Crane

Front cover photos: © Royalty-Free/CORBIS

Printed in China through Colorcraft Ltd., Hong Kong

Printing History
1st edition—June 2003
5 4 3 2 1

Please send all comments, corrections, additions, amendments, and critiques to:

Moon Metro Rome
Avalon Travel Publishing
1400 65th Street, Suite 250
Emeryville, CA 94608, USA
email: atpfeedback@avalonpub.com
website: www.moon.com

PHOTO CREDITS

© Folio, Inc: Page 10 Musei Vatican/Cappall

Philip Shipman: Map 1 Forno di Campo; Map 1 Vineria; Map 1 Viola; Map 1 (outer flap) Campo dei Fiori; Map 2 Santa Maria Sopra Minerva; Map 2 Hotel Raphael; Map 2 Johnathan's Angels; Map 2 Sangallo; Map 2 The Gallery; Map 2 (outer flap) Piazza Navona; Map 2 (outer flap) Tazza D'Oro; Map 2 (outer flap) Pantheon; Map 3 Il Gelato di San Crispino; Map 3 Gilda; Map 3 Galleria Nazionale D'Arte Antica; Map 3 Reef; Map 3 Federico Buccellati; Map 3 (outer flap) Fontana di Trevi; Map 3 (outer flap) Villa Borghese; Map 3 (outer flap) Antico Café Greco; Map 4 Scooters; Map 4 Feltrinelli International; Map 4 Teatro dell Opera di Roma; Map 4 Piazza Della Republica; Map 4 (outer flap) Galleria Borghese; Map 4 (outer flap) Quattro Fontane; Map 4 (outer flap) Santa Maria Maggiore; Map 5 Foro Romano; Map 5 Ricordi; Map 5 Galleria Doria Pamphili; Map 5 Museo di Palazzo Venezia; Map 5 Arc di Constantino; Map 5 (outer flap) Colosseo; Map 6 Teatro Belli; Map 6 Ombre Rosse; Map 6 Scala Quattordici; Map 6 Museo di Roma in trastevere; Map 6 Hotel Ripa; Map 6 (outer flap) Santa Maria in Trastevere; Map 6 (outer flap) The Corner Bookshop; Map 6 (outer flap) Teatro Belli; Map 7 Museo Storico Nazionale Dell Arte Sanitaria; Map 7 Villa Farnesina; Map 7 Fonclea; Map 7 La Veranda Dell Hotel Columbus; Map 7 Along the Tiber; Map 7 (outer flap) Castel Sant' Angelo; Map 7 (outer flap) Basilica di San Pietro; Map 7 (outer flap) Museo Napoleonico; Overview MAP Enoteca Ferrara; Overview MAP Orto Botanica; Overview MAP Valzani; Overview MAP The Corner Bookshop; Overview MAP (outer left flap) Basilica di San Pietro; Overview MAP (outer right flap) Piazza Venezia; Page 02 Basilica di San Pietro; Page 02 Fonclea; Page 02 La Veranda Dell Hotel Columbus; Page 02 Pont Sant Angelo; Page 02 Constantini; Page 03 Campo dei Fiori; Page 04 Castel Sant' Angelo; Page 06 Catacombs; Page 07 Colosseo; Page 08 Femme Sistina; Page 08 Gilda; Page 08 La Terrazza Dell 'Eden; Page 08 Antico Café Greco; Page 09 Fontana di Trevi; Page 10 Foro di Traiano; Page 10 I Vitelloni; Page 10 Domus Aurea; Page 10 Galleria Doria Pamphili; Page 10 La Corte; Page 11 Foro Romano; Page 13 Pantheon; Page 14 Piazza Del Campidoglio; Page 17 Piazza di Spagna; Page 18 Piazza Navona; Page 19 San Clemente; Page 20 Santa Maria in Trastevere; Page 20 Enoteca Ferrara; Page 20 Orto Botanica; Page 20 Valzani; Page 20 The Corner Bookshop; Page 21 Terme Di Caracalla; Page 22 Villa Borghese; Page 26 Antico Café; Page 27 Bablngton's Tea Rooms; Page 27 Il Dacaro; Page 28 Campo; Page 29 Da Checco ei Carettiere; Page 29 Ditlrambo; Page 30 Enoteca Ferrara; Page 30 Forno; Page 30 Il Gelato di San Crispino; Page 31 Monte Caruso; Page 32 Ombre Rosse; Page 33 Reef; Page 34 Sangallo; Page 35 Tazza D'Oro; Page 36 La Veranda Dell Hotel Columbus; Page 36 Valzani; Page 36 Vineria; Page 40 Anglo-American Books; Page 40 Antica Erboristeria Romana; Page 40 AVC; Page 40 Battistoni; Page 41 Best Seller; Page 41 Brighenti; Page 41 Bulgari; Page 42 Constantini; Page 42 Dolce & Gabbana; Page 42 The Corner Bookshop; Page 43 Fausto Santani; Page 43 Federico Buccellati; Page 43 Feltrinelli International; Page 43 Femme Sistina; Page 44 Hedy Martinelli; Page 45 Loco; Page 46 Il Papiro; Page 46 O Testa; Page 46 Polvere di Tempo; Page 47 Ricordi; Page 47 Rinascita; Page 47 Scala Quattordici; Page 47 Sergio Valente Beauty Center; Page 48 Tods; Page 48 Viola; Page 50 Galleria Borghese; Page 50 Galleria Doria Pamphilia; Page 50 Galleria Nazionale D'Arte Antica; Page 51 Museo Del Corso; Page 52 Museo di Roma in Trastevere; Page 52 Museo Napoleonico; Page 52 Museo Nazionale Romano Palazzo Altemps; Page 53 Museo Storico Nazionale Dell Arte Sanitaria; Page 53 Palazzo Corsini; Page 53 Villa Farnesina; Page 54 Teatro Belli; Page 54 Teatro di Roma Argentina; Page 55 Teatro Dell Opera; Page 55 Teatro Flaiano; Page 55 Teatro XX Secolo; Page 56 Anima; Page 56 Fonclea; Page 56 Gilda; Page 57 The Drunken Ship; Page 57 The Gallery; Page 58 I Vitelloni; Page 58 Johnathan's Angels; Page 59 Arc di Constantino; Page 59 Chiesa Del Gesu; Page 59 Circo Massimo; Page 59 Domus aurea; Page 60 Gianicolo; Page 60 Il Galappatoio; Page 60 Oro Botanico; Page 61 Piazza del Popolo; Page 61 Piazza Republic; Page 61 Quattro Fontane; Page 62 Santa Maria Sopra Minerva; Page 62 Scooters; Page 64 Ripa; Page 65 Cavalieri Hilton; Page 66 Gregoriana Hotel; Page 67 Hotel Raphael

MOON METRO

- AMSTERDAM
- BERLIN
- CHICAGO
- LONDON
- LOS ANGELES
- NEW YORK CITY
- PARIS
- ROME
- SAN FRANCISCO
- SEATTLE
- TORONTO
- WASHINGTON D.C.

**AVAILABLE AT YOUR FAVORITE
BOOK AND TRAVEL STORES**

UNFOLD THE CITY

MOON METRO
CHICAGO

MOON METRO
LOS ANGELES

MOON METRO
LONDON

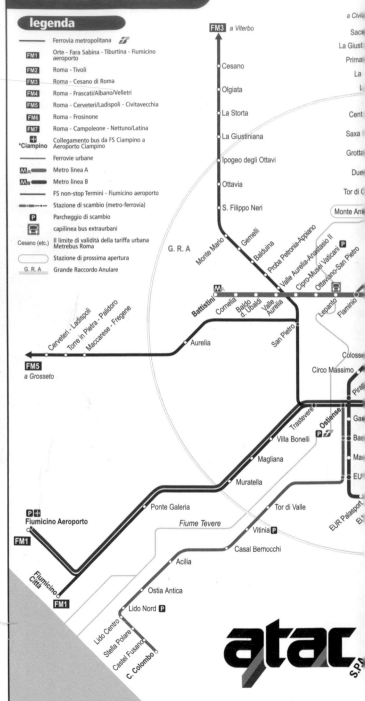